Unleashing Your Inner Titan: Mastering Self-Discipline For Men

Harness Your Willpower, Achieve Success, and Forge an Indomitable Spirit

ASHLEY ROYCE

TABLE OF CONTENTS

INTRODUCTION

We live in a tough world. We're supposed to be everything all at once, without having the time to stop and ask ourselves what we really want. If we admit that we sometimes don't feel worthy or strong enough to face whatever life throws at us, it's seen as a weakness.

But is there a better way?

It doesn't matter who you are, what you do, or how old you are, it's never too late to stop, take stock, and change your life for the better.

Now, I know, it sounds like a cheesy movie, but the truth is, if you want to be happy in your life, and reach your potential, you need to harness the power within you. Every man has an inner titan waiting to be unleashed. It's not some chest-thumping giant or a Viking-esque character, but a quiet strength that allows you to push through life's challenges and reach your goals.

Of course, you can choose to take the easy route. You can sit down, decide that life doesn't want you to excel, and carry on the way you are. If that's what you want to do, well, you're not about to get very far. You really might as well just give up. However, if you have an inner desire for more, you've come to the right place.

The truth is that life isn't going to drop everything you want into your lap; it's going to take time, effort, and some hard graft. But you're good with that, right? Nothing in life comes to those who sit around and expect it to be given to them; if you want something, you have to go out there and get it. Your inner titan is the one who does the work.

By allowing this shadowy figure into your life, you're realize your worth. For the first time, you'll understand that you are enough, you can do whatever you want, and be whatever you want to be. By harnessing your inner power, you can manifest everything you want in life thanks to your strength of character and willpower to help you through.

No magic required.

"Unleashing Your Inner Titan: Mastering Self-Discipline for Men" is more than just a guide; it is a roadmap to harnessing your willpower and forging an indomitable spirit. In this compelling odyssey of personal growth, we delve deep into the core of self-discipline, empowering you to break free from the shackles of self-doubt and embrace the commanding authority that awaits. Once you do that, anything is possible.

The only question you need to ask yourself is whether you're prepared to embark upon this journey and fight through the barriers you will face along the way.

So, are you?

You're about to learn how to summon your inner strength, command your impulses, and channel your passions toward a singular purpose: achieving unparalleled success in everything you do, no matter how big or small.

Yes, it sounds like a mountain to climb, and in many ways, it is. Your inner titan isn't interested in the easy route; he's a brute, a force of nature, and he sees a challenge with a glint in his eye. He knows he can overcome whatever life throws at him because he's got the will to be successful, even in the face of difficulties.

Right now, that guy doesn't sound like you. I get it. But you can develop all of this and more if you simply take the time to look within, be brave enough to smash through your preconceived notions, and embrace the journey to self-transformation.

Are you ready?

CHAPTER 1

You Can't Succeed Without Self-Discipline

Whether you know it right now or not, deep within the core of your being lies an extraordinary force, a power so immense that it has the potential to reshape your entire existence. This force is what we call your inner titan.

Imagine a mythical titan—an embodiment of strength, resilience, and unyielding determination. It stands tall, radiating an aura of unwavering power. But your inner titan is not a distant myth or a figment of imagination. It is a living, breathing part of who you are, patiently awaiting recognition and liberation. He's asleep, snoozing, waiting for you to shake him and push him out of bed.

Embracing your inner titan means embracing the essence of your true potential. It is about unleashing the raw power that resides within you, shattering the chains of self-doubt, and awakening a spirit that refuses to be confined. Your inner titan calls upon you to seize every opportunity, to conquer your fears, and to forge an unbreakable path toward your dreams.

Your inner titan is a relentless warrior, fearless in the face of adversity. He knows that challenges are not roadblocks but stepping stones on the path to triumph. He thrives on perseverance, refusing to succumb to setbacks or obstacles. With your inner titan by your side, failure becomes a mere detour, redirecting you towards a greater victory.

The first step is to let go of self-imposed limitations and embrace the extraordinary power that resides within. Then, fully embrace your inner titan; it is the catalyst that will propel you toward greatness.

The first step toward doing all of that? Self-discipline.

Self-Discipline Is Your Friend

Imagine waking up each day, driven by an inner fire that refuses to be extinguished. You might want to stay in bed for an extra ten minutes, but something pushes you to get up, grab a coffee, and start the day with extreme focus and attention.

That's self-discipline calling.

With self-discipline, you become the captain of your destiny, charting a course toward your dreams with unwavering resolve. It is the force that compels you to take action, to stay focused even when distractions beg for your attention.

The truth is, you won't get very far in life if you don't develop self-discipline to push you through those times when you'd rather do anything but the one thing that's going to get you where you need to be.

Your inner titan is a self-disciplined character, so first, you need to understand the concept and work toward achieving it.

What Does Self-Discipline Look Like?

Self-discipline is a crucial trait that every man should strive to develop in his life. It is the ability to control your impulses, emotions, and actions in order to achieve long-term goals and lead a fulfilling life. Self-discipline requires commitment, focus, and perseverance, but the rewards it brings are immeasurable.

One of the first key aspects of self-discipline for men is maintaining physical fitness. Regular exercise and healthy eating habits are essential for overall well-being. By practicing self-discipline in this area, you can maintain a healthy weight, improve your strength and endurance, and reduce the risk of various health issues such as heart disease or diabetes.

In addition to physical fitness, self-discipline plays a significant role in professional success. Men who possess self-discipline are more likely to set clear goals for their careers and work diligently towards achieving them. They have the ability to prioritize tasks effectively, manage their time efficiently, and stay focused on their objectives even when faced with distractions or setbacks.

Self-disciplined men also tend to be more organized in all aspects of life. They create routines that help them stay on track with daily responsibilities such as household chores or financial management. By developing good organizational skills through self-discipline, you can reduce stress levels and ensure that you have enough time for both work-related commitments and personal interests.

Finally, self-discipline also encompasses self-control. It involves managing your emotions effectively by not letting anger or frustration dictate your actions or decisions. Self-controlled individuals think before they act; they consider the consequences of their behavior before responding impulsively.

Moreover, practicing self-control allows men to resist temptations that may hinder progress towards long-term goals. We're talking about willpower here. Whether it's avoiding unhealthy habits like excessive drinking or smoking or resisting short-term pleasures like procrastination or indulging in unhealthy foods regularly, having strong willpower enables you to make better choices for yourself.

It is important to note that developing self-discipline takes time and effort; it is not something that happens overnight. However, with determination and consistent practice of self-control techniques such as goal-setting, time management strategies or mindfulness exercises, any man can become more disciplined over time. Yes, even you!

Remember that self-discipline is not about being rigid or denying yourself enjoyment; rather it's about making conscious choices that align with long-term goals while still finding joy in the journey towards achieving them.

Developing Self-Discipline

Now you know what self-discipline is all about, how can you start to implement it into your life?

This whole process will take time and you might have a few stumbles along the way. It's okay. Your inner titan doesn't mind the odd mistake from time to time, as long as you learn from it and do better next time.

Let's take a look at some of the key aspects to help you develop a strong sense of self-discipline.

Habit Formation

Cultivating positive habits can streamline self-discipline efforts. Repeatedly practicing desired behaviors turns them into automatic responses, reducing the reliance on willpower alone. Over time, your responses will simply happen instinctively.

There are a few key components to habit formation. First, there is a cue or trigger that initiates the behavior. This could be something external, like a specific time of day or an environmental cue, or it could be internal, such as an emotion or a thought.

Once the cue is present, you engage in the behavior itself. This is where repetition comes into play. By consistently performing the behavior in response to the cue, you reinforce its association and strengthen neural pathways in your brain.

The third component is reward. When you engage in a habit and experience some form of positive reinforcement or satisfaction afterward, your brain releases dopamine—a neurotransmitter associated with pleasure and motivation. This reinforces the habit loop and increases your likelihood of repeating it in similar situations.

To form new habits effectively, it can be helpful to start small with achievable goals and gradually increase difficulty over time. Consistency is key; repeating behaviors regularly helps solidify them into habits more quickly.

Remember that breaking old habits can also be challenging but not impossible! By identifying triggers for unwanted behaviors and replacing them with healthier alternatives while staying motivated through rewards (even small ones), you can successfully replace old patterns with new ones.

Mindfulness and Meditation

Mindfulness and meditation are powerful tools that can greatly contribute to developing self-discipline. By practicing mindfulness, you cultivate a heightened awareness of your thoughts, emotions, and actions in the present moment. This increased awareness allows you to better understand your patterns of behavior and make conscious choices about how to respond to various situations.

When it comes to self-discipline, mindfulness helps you recognize the impulses and distractions that often lead you astray from your goals. By being fully present in each moment, you can observe these distractions without judgment or attachment, allowing them to pass by without derailing your focus.

Meditation is another valuable practice for developing self-discipline. Through regular meditation sessions, we train our minds to stay focused on a single point of attention (such as the breath or a mantra) while letting go of any wandering thoughts or external distractions. This ability to maintain focus translates directly into improved discipline in other areas of life.

Moreover, meditation helps reduce stress levels and enhances emotional regulation skills. When faced with challenges or temptations that might normally trigger impulsive behavior or procrastination, you're more likely to pause and respond thoughtfully rather than react impulsively.

Environment and Triggers

Developing self-discipline can be challenging, especially when faced with environmental factors and triggers that may hinder your progress. However, with the right strategies and mindset, you can overcome these obstacles. Here are some helpful tips:

- **Identify your triggers:** Start by recognizing the specific situations or stimuli that tend to derail your self-discipline efforts. It could be certain people, places, or even emotions that make it harder for you to stay focused and disciplined.

- **Create a supportive environment:** Modify your surroundings to support your goals rather than hinder them. For example, if you're trying to develop a habit of studying regularly but find yourself easily distracted at home, consider going to a library or coffee shop where you can concentrate better.

- **Set clear goals:** Clearly define what you want to achieve and why it is important to you. Having a strong sense of purpose will help motivate you during challenging times.

- **Break tasks into smaller steps:** Sometimes the sheer size of a task can feel overwhelming and lead to procrastination or loss of focus. Break down larger tasks into smaller, more manageable steps so that they seem less daunting.

- **Use positive reinforcement:** Reward yourself for small victories along the way as this helps reinforce positive behavior patterns and motivates further progress.
- **Find an accountability partner:** Share your goals with someone who will hold you accountable for staying disciplined in achieving them—a friend, family member, or even an online community dedicated to similar objectives.
- **Seek support from others:** Surround yourself with like-minded individuals who are also working on developing their self-discipline skills; their encouragement and shared experiences can be invaluable.
- **Be kind to yourself:** Remember that developing self-discipline is a journey, and setbacks are normal. If you slip up or face challenges, don't beat yourself up; instead, learn from the experience and use it as an opportunity for growth.

Debunking Common Misconceptions About Self-Discipline

It's possible that you have the entirely wrong idea about self-discipline, and it might stop you from going out there and achieving what you want. So, before we move on, let's debunk some of the most common myths and misconceptions about self-discipline. That way, you're on the right page from the get-go.

Misconception #1: Self-discipline is innate, reserved for the chosen few

Self-discipline is not an exclusive gift bestowed upon a select few at birth. It is a skill that can be cultivated and nurtured by anyone who dares to embark on the journey of self-improvement.

Misconception #2: Self-discipline is rigid and joyless

Not at all! Self-discipline is not a stern taskmaster, draining joy from life's endeavors. When you embrace self-discipline, you liberate yourself from the chains of distraction and procrastination. Self-discipline becomes the wings that carries you to heights of fulfillment and joy previously unimaginable.

Misconception #3: Self-discipline requires perfection

Self-discipline does not demand flawless execution or an unblemished record of achievements. It acknowledges your humanity and recognizes that missteps and setbacks are an integral part of the journey. You're human, after all.

Self-discipline invites you to learn from your mistakes, to grow stronger through resilience, and to persist in the face of adversity. It is the steadfast commitment to progress, not perfection, that fuels the fires of self-discipline.

Misconception #4: Self-discipline stifles creativity and spontaneity

Self-discipline is not the enemy of creativity and spontaneity. To the contrary, it's their steadfast ally. It provides the structure and focus that allows your creative energies to flow freely and your spontaneous moments to flourish.

Misconception #5: Self-discipline is a solitary endeavor

Self-discipline does not require you to journey alone. In fact, the support and accountability of like-minded individuals can amplify your discipline and accelerate your progress. By surrounding yourself with a community of people with shared aspirations, you find strength, encouragement, and the collective wisdom to navigate the challenges that arise.

Remember, developing self-discipline takes time and effort. It's not going to come your way overnight, but with perseverance and awareness, it will come your way. Self-discipline is a key factor of growth and development and without it, you're not going to get where you want to be. But with it, anything is possible.

CHAPTER 2

Cultivating a Mindset of Strength, Determination, & Resilience

Throughout our lives, we often face challenges and adversities that test our ability to cope and persevere. It happens to everyone yet doesn't make it any easier to deal with in the heat of the moment. Cultivating a mindset of strength, resilience, and determination is essential to overcome obstacles, achieve personal growth, and thrive in the face of adversity.

This specific mindset involves a combination of psychological strategies and attitudes that can be developed and strengthened over time. Let's call this your 'Inner Titan Mindset.'

So, how can you start using this mindset for your greater good and tap into its abundant strength?

Embrace a Growth Mindset

A growth mindset is the belief that your abilities and intelligence can be developed through dedication, effort, and learning. It is the understanding that talents and skills can be cultivated over time, rather than being fixed traits.

It can be difficult to switch from a fixed mindset, when you believe that everything happens *to* you without any control, to a growth mindset where anything is possible. However, always ask yourself what can be done to make a situation better. Try to see the glass as half full, rather than half empty, and look for the silver lining in everything.

Remember, developing a growth mindset is an ongoing process that requires patience, self-reflection, and consistent practice. It won't come to you overnight, but it will slowly start to creep into your life and stick around.

Develop Self-Awareness

Understanding your emotions, strengths, weaknesses, and triggers is crucial for building resilience. Self-awareness allows you to recognize your emotional responses to challenges and empowers you to respond constructively instead of reacting impulsively.

Journaling is a great way to become more aware of your thoughts, feelings, and triggers. It's also a good idea to accept feedback from other people and try to show empathy to others as much as possible. These are all ways you can become more aware of yourself. And if you make a mistake, don't allow it to drag you down. Your inner titan embraces failure as a learning curve, so whenever you feel like you've made a mistake, look at what you can learn, and go again.

Build Emotional Resilience

Emotional resilience is the ability to bounce back from setbacks and manage stress effectively. Developing emotional intelligence and coping skills enables you to navigate difficult situations without being overwhelmed by negative emotions.

Self-awareness ties in very closely to emotional resilience because it gives you insights into what triggers your emotions and how you deal with it. Again, journaling is a good tool here, and addressing any hidden issues that cause you to feel negatively about life.

Focus on Positive Thinking

Cultivating a positive mindset does not mean ignoring challenges, but rather adopting an optimistic outlook and seeking solutions. Positive thinking can boost motivation and help maintain determination during tough times.

Whenever you recognize that you're thinking negatively, try to reframe it to something positive and then repeat it as a mantra. Over time, the positive will slowly replace the negative and you'll start to see that point before the doom and gloom. You can also try positive affirmations to reset your brain toward the sunnier side of life.

Set Realistic Goals

Establishing clear, achievable goals provides direction and purpose. Break larger goals into smaller, manageable tasks, which can enhance a sense of progress and accomplishment along your path.

Goals should be SMART (specific, measurable, achievable, relevant, and time-bound). Following this allows you to choose goals that you can reach and not ones that force you to set yourself up for failure before you've even begun. Remember to celebrate every goal achieved before setting another.

Learn from Failures and Setbacks

Viewing failures as learning opportunities rather than personal shortcomings fosters resilience. Analyzing setbacks, extracting valuable lessons, and adjusting strategies accordingly can lead to eventual success.

Of course, it's disappointing when you feel like you've failed at something, but you're human and it's important that you stop being so hard on yourself. Every single person on the planet makes mistakes and while it's not pleasant to admit, there is a lesson in every single thing that goes wrong. Find the insights and then move forward, never ignoring what you've learned.

Practice Gratitude

Gratitude cultivates a positive mindset by focusing on the blessings and positive aspects of life. Acknowledging and appreciating the good can strengthen resilience during challenging times.

A gratitude journal is a good tool to help cultivate this skill. Every evening, write down three things you're grateful for from that particular day. It can be as small as a coffee you really enjoyed or seeing a friend you've not seen for a long time. After a few weeks, read your journal back and see how much good you have in your life, and what you have to be grateful for.

Cultivate a Supportive Network

Surrounding yourself with supportive and like-minded individuals provides a valuable source of encouragement and understanding. A strong support system can bolster determination and resilience. Just because you're becoming a titan, doesn't mean you have to do everything alone. There is strength in numbers, after all.

Embrace Change and Adaptability

Life is full of unexpected twists, and the ability to adapt to new circumstances is vital for building resilience. Embrace change as an opportunity for growth and approach it with a flexible mindset.

Just because you may not know how to do something or a situation is new to you, doesn't mean it can't become one of your strengths. Face every challenge with the idea that you're about to learn something new. And if you need to ask for help, don't be afraid to do so. You don't have to do everything in life on your own.

Developing Unshakeable Belief in Yourself

Deep within the core of your being, there exists a reservoir of untapped capabilities and boundless courage, yearning to break free from the shackles of doubt. With this, you have the ability to sculpt your destiny and shape your reality.

Put simply, believing in yourself is not just a box to be ticked; it is the driving force that propels dreamers to become doers, and the beacon that guides you through the darkest nights, illuminating a path to greatness. But how can you nurture this ember of belief into an inferno of unshakeable confidence?

Here are some steps you can take to develop self-belief:

- **Identify your strengths:** Take some time to reflect on your skills, talents, and accomplishments. Recognize what you excel at and what makes you unique. Focusing on your strengths will help boost your confidence.
- **Set realistic goals:** Break down big goals into smaller, achievable ones. By setting realistic goals, you can experience small wins along the way, which will reinforce your belief in yourself.
- **Challenge negative thoughts:** Pay attention to any negative thoughts or self-doubt that may arise in your mind. We all have negative thoughts about ourselves from time to time but it's important to replace them with positive affirmations or counterarguments that support your abilities and potential.
- **Surround yourself with positivity:** Surround yourself with supportive and positive people who believe in you and encourage your growth. Avoid individuals who bring negativity or doubt into your life.
- **Celebrate successes:** Acknowledge and celebrate even the smallest achievements along the way towards reaching

your goals. This will reinforce a positive mindset and build confidence in yourself.

- **Learn from failures:** Instead of viewing failures as setbacks, see them as opportunities for growth and learning experiences. Analyze what went wrong, make adjustments if needed, and move forward with newfound knowledge.
- **Practice self-care:** Taking care of yourself physically, mentally, emotionally, and spiritually is crucial for building self-belief. Engage in activities that bring you joy, practice mindfulness or meditation techniques to calm the mind, and exercise regularly to boost endorphins—all of these activities contribute to a healthy sense of self-worth.
- **Accept imperfections:** Understand that nobody is perfect. Everyone has flaws or makes mistakes at times; it's part of being human! Embrace imperfections as opportunities for growth rather than reasons for self-doubt.
- **Seek feedback from trusted sources:** Reach out to mentors or trusted friends/family members who can provide constructive feedback and guidance. Their input can help you gain a fresh perspective on your abilities and areas for improvement.

The more you practice these elements, the more you'll notice a strong belief in yourself developing. Remember, there is only one of you, and you have a huge amount of value to bring to the world. All of that starts from within.

CHAPTER 3

You're Right on Time

Time management is a crucial aspect of self-development that often gets overlooked. It involves planning and organizing your time effectively to achieve your goals and make the most out of every day. By managing your time wisely, you can increase productivity, reduce stress, and create a better work-life balance.

Your inner titan does not want to be late. If you're always rushing around and never making time for the things that matter, not only do your relationships suffer, but everything else in your life is pushed onto the back burner. You're creating the perfect situation for stress to enter the fore.

One of the main reasons why time management is important in self-development is because it allows you to prioritize tasks and activities based on their importance and urgency. When you have a clear plan for how to spend your time, you can focus on what truly matters and avoid wasting precious moments on unimportant or trivial things. This helps you stay focused, motivated, and efficient in achieving your personal or professional goals.

Of course, we mentioned stress, and effective time management helps reduce stress levels. When you feel overwhelmed by an endless list of tasks or deadlines looming over you, it's easy to become anxious or frustrated. However, by breaking down your workload into manageable chunks and allocating specific times for each task, you can approach them with a calmer mindset. This not only enhances your ability to concentrate but also gives you a sense of control over your responsibilities.

Time management also plays a significant role in creating a healthy work-life balance. In today's fast-paced world where we are constantly bombarded with demands from work, family obligations, social commitments, and hobbies, finding equilibrium between these areas can be challenging. By effectively managing your time, you can allocate sufficient hours for work while still making room for personal pursuits that bring joy and fulfillment into your life.

Moreover, good time management cultivates discipline and self-discipline is an essential trait for personal growth, something needed for your inner titan to be released into the world. It requires setting boundaries around distractions such as excessive use of social media or procrastination habits that hinder progress towards achieving your goals. By consciously choosing how you spend each moment throughout the day instead of letting external factors dictate it for you, you take charge of shaping your own destiny.

Techniques for Prioritizing Tasks and Slaying Time-Wasting Dragons

It's very easy to become bogged down with tasks that aren't that important, and by focusing upon them, you're wasting time. Instead, you need to learn to focus on the most urgent or important task first and work your way down from there.

So, how can you do that?

- **The art of prioritization:** Picture yourself as a conductor of a magnificent symphony, each task an instrument, waiting to play its part. Prioritization is the art of orchestrating this dance, recognizing the crescendos of importance and cadences of urgency. A good way to prioritize is to write down all the tasks you need to do that day and number them in order of urgency/importance. Start with the most urgent and tick tasks off as you go.

- **The Eisenhower Matrix:** The Eisenhower Matrix involves dividing your tasks into four quadrants. For tasks in the "Important and Urgent" section, take action. In "Important but Not Urgent," cultivate proactive planning and preparation. Embrace "Urgent but Not Important" with a discerning eye, delegating or minimizing wherever possible. As for the "Not Important and Not Urgent," bid those tasks farewell with grace.
- **The Pareto Principle:** The Pareto Principle says that 80% of outcomes emerge from 20% of efforts. Embrace this empowering wisdom and channel your energy toward the vital few tasks that yield the greatest impact.
- **The power of NO:** Amidst the endless demands of life, the power of "NO" emerges as a shield of self-respect. Empower yourself to graciously decline time-wasting invitations and distractions that do not align with your priorities. Embrace the freedom that comes with setting boundaries; it opens the door to profound focus and achievement. It might take some practice at first, as we're all so used to saying "yes" as much as we can, but "no" is just as vital.
- **Tame the temptation of distractions:** The dragons of distractions may roar, but fear not, for you hold the sword of discipline! Create an environment that shields you from temptation. Silence the siren calls of social media, summon your focus amidst the chaos, and immerse yourself in the flow of undistracted work. It's a good idea to keep your phone on silent and block notifications from your social media feeds.

Also, avoid checking your emails too often; once in the morning, once at lunch time, and once before you sign off for the day is enough.

- **The many benefits of time blocking:** Dedicate specific time slots for designated tasks, allowing your mind to flow effortlessly from one job to the next. By embracing time blocking, you unleash the potential of uninterrupted focus.
- **Mindful YES:** As you learn to say "YES" to what truly matters, bask in the gentle grace of mindfulness. Engage in each task with complete presence, savoring the journey and relishing the small triumphs. In the act of embracing the moment, you discover the true essence of fulfillment and joy.

These time management techniques are very easy to incorporate into your day, and with regular practice, you'll slowly start to notice you have more time than ever before. Of course, what you choose to do with that time is your decision, but make sure you choose wisely!

Strategies for Overcoming Procrastination and Staying Focused

Procrastination is the act of delaying or postponing tasks or actions that need to be done, often resulting in unnecessary stress and a last-minute rush to complete them. It's like putting off something today that you could do tomorrow, and then repeating the cycle.

Most of us procrastinate from time to time but when it becomes a regular habit, it can stand between you and your goals. The good news is that there are some powerful strategies to help kick procrastination out of your life for good.

- **Understand the roots of procrastination:** To combat procrastination effectively, you must first delve into its origins. Recognize the underlying factors contributing to your procrastination—whether it's fear of failure, perfectionism, lack of clarity, or simply a lack of motivation. Identifying these triggers empowers you to address them directly and develop targeted strategies for each challenge.

- **Set clear goals and prioritize:** Remember, goals serve as your North Star of focus. Clearly define your objectives and break them down into actionable steps. Prioritize these tasks based on their importance and urgency. A clear roadmap allows you to navigate the journey with purpose and direction.
- **Utilize the Two-Minute Rule:** The Two-Minute Rule, a powerful ally against procrastination, says that if a task can be completed in two minutes or less, do it immediately. By accomplishing quick and easy tasks promptly, you gain momentum and set the tone for greater productivity.
- **Use the Pomodoro Technique:** The Pomodoro Technique, a time management method, involves working in short, focused intervals (typically 25 minutes), followed by a brief break. Embrace the ebb and flow of these intervals, as they optimize productivity and prevent burnout. This is a proven technique to get rid of procrastination for good.
- **Employ visualization techniques:** Envision the fruits of your labor and immerse yourself in the excitement of achieving your goals. Visualization techniques amplify your motivation and help you overcome mental barriers that lead to procrastination. Picture yourself having completed your daily to-do list and imagine how it feels.
- **Create a distraction-free environment:** Create an environment that minimizes distractions and maximizes focus. Clear clutter, silence notifications, and set boundaries to protect your designated workspaces from time-wasting intruders.

- **Break tasks into smaller steps:** Large tasks can be overwhelming, leading to procrastination. Divide them into smaller, manageable steps, and celebrate progress at each milestone. The satisfaction of completing these mini-goals fuels your motivation to tackle the next step.
- **Cultivate accountability:** Share your goals with an accountability partner or a supportive community. Knowing that others are cheering for your success encourages you to stay focused and committed.
- **Practice self-compassion:** Be kind to yourself and acknowledge that occasional lapses in focus are part of the human experience. Instead of berating yourself for moments of procrastination, gently redirect your focus toward your goals.
- **Imagine tomorrow:** At the moment of procrastination, ask yourself how you'll feel tomorrow when you have twice as much work to do. It could be all it takes to push you to complete that task.

Time management plays a crucial role in personal development by helping you prioritize your tasks, achieve goals, and maintain a healthy work-life balance. It will boost your productivity, help you work toward and achieve your goals, reduce stress levels, and help you make stronger decisions.

CHAPTER 4

Strengthen That Willpower Muscle

Do you have willpower?

Think about it for a second. Do you find it easy to keep going when life throws you curveballs, or do you tend to give in at the first sign of trouble? Or, if you know you can't have something, do you go for it anyway, or do you stick with the sensible route?

These are all examples of situations when willpower is a must. The problem is, many of us struggle with it, not realizing that we need to give our willpower muscles a work out from time to time.

Willpower is the ability to control and direct your thoughts, actions, and behaviors toward achieving a desired goal or outcome. It is often referred to as self-discipline or self-control. Willpower allows you to resist immediate gratification in favor of long-term benefits.

Willpower is important for several reasons:

- **Goal Achievement:** Willpower helps you stay focused and committed to your goals, even when faced with obstacles or distractions. It enables you to overcome challenges and persist in your efforts until you achieve success.

- **Self-Improvement:** With willpower, you can make positive changes in your life by breaking bad habits, adopting healthier lifestyles, and acquiring new skills. It empowers you to make choices that align with your long-term well-being.
- **Resisting Temptation:** Willpower helps you resist impulsive behaviors that may have negative consequences. It allows you to delay gratification and make more rational decisions rather than succumbing to immediate desires.
- **Emotional Regulation:** Willpower plays a crucial role in managing emotions effectively. It helps you control impulsive reactions during stressful situations, allowing for better decision-making and maintaining healthy relationships.
- **Productivity and Success:** Strong willpower enhances productivity by enabling you to stay focused on tasks without getting easily distracted or procrastinating. This leads to increased efficiency and ultimately contributes to personal success.

Remember that willpower is like a muscle, which means that it can be strengthened through consistent practice. However, it is not an infinite resource; it can be depleted over time through decision-making and self-control efforts. The phenomenon of "ego depletion" or "willpower depletion" suggests that the mental exertion required for self-discipline can lead to decreased self-control in subsequent tasks. This highlights the importance of managing willpower reserves wisely and replenishing them through rest and self-care.

Developing Willpower

Willpower can be strengthened and honed through intentional practice. Engaging in exercises that challenge self-control, such as avoiding temptations, setting and achieving goals, and managing time effectively, can help build resilience and enhance self-discipline.

Of course, motivation acts as a fuel for willpower and self-discipline. When you are intrinsically motivated by your values, passions, or personal aspirations, you experience heightened self-control and perseverance. Cultivating a sense of purpose and connecting actions to meaningful goals enhances the capacity for self-discipline.

The Interplay with Habits

Habits interact with willpower and self-discipline. When habits align with desired goals, they reduce the reliance on willpower, making self-discipline easier to maintain. Intentionally cultivating positive habits can become a powerful ally in the journey toward self-control.

Willpower also empowers you to resist the allure of instant gratification in favor of delayed rewards or long-term benefits. By adopting a future-oriented mindset and envisioning the rewards of self-discipline, you become better equipped to overcome immediate temptations.

Techniques for Boosting Willpower by Resisting Temptation

If you're someone who struggles with willpower, the good news is that there are practical techniques you can employ to boost your willpower and fortify your ability to stay on track even when faced with distractions and temptations.

- **Set clear and specific goals:** Begin by defining clear and specific goals. When you have a clear vision of what you want to achieve, it becomes easier to align your actions with your long-term aspirations. This clarity of purpose serves as a driving force behind your willpower.
- **Break goals into smaller steps:** Breaking down your goals into smaller, manageable steps makes them less overwhelming and more achievable. This approach helps you build momentum

and maintain focus, as each small victory contributes to your overall progress.

- **Connect with intrinsic motivation:** Understand the deeper reasons and values behind your goals. When you are intrinsically motivated, meaning you genuinely find value and meaning in your pursuits, your willpower is strengthened as you connect emotionally with your objectives.
- **Develop positive habits:** Habits, once established, require less willpower to maintain. Cultivate positive habits that support your goals, as they become automatic actions, reducing the need for continuous self-control.
- **Practice mindfulness:** Mindfulness cultivates self-awareness, enabling you to recognize temptations as they arise and make conscious decisions in the moment. Being present and mindful of your thoughts and impulses empower you to respond intentionally, rather than reactively.
- **Create accountability:** As always, remember to share your goals and progress with a trusted friend, family member, or support group. Accountability provides external motivation and encouragement, reinforcing your commitment to stay on course.
- **Avoid or minimize temptations:** Whenever possible, limit exposure to situations or environments that trigger temptations. By minimizing potential distractions, you reduce the strain on your willpower reserves. If you're not sure what your triggers are, keeping a journal will help you identify them.
- **Celebrate small victories:** Acknowledge and celebrate your achievements, even the minor ones. Celebrating small victories boosts morale and reinforces the link between effort and reward, making you more likely to persevere.

- **Practice self-compassion:** Acknowledge that setbacks and mistakes are a natural part of the human experience. Avoid self-criticism and practice self-compassion, treating yourself with kindness and understanding.
- **Prioritize rest and self-care:** Willpower can be depleted by mental and physical fatigue. Ensure you get enough sleep, engage in regular exercise, and take breaks when needed to recharge your willpower reserves.
- **Implement intentions:** Create "if-then" plans to anticipate and prepare for challenging situations. For example, "If I feel tempted to indulge in unhealthy snacks, then I will have a nutritious alternative ready."
- **Learn from slip-ups:** Instead of viewing lapses in willpower as failures, see them as opportunities for learning and growth. Identify the triggers and circumstances that led to the slip-up and strategize ways to handle similar situations in the future.

Incorporating these techniques into your daily life allows you to cultivate stronger willpower and a greater ability to resist temptations.

Building Resilience & Perseverance in the Face of Challenges

Resilience and perseverance are essential traits that empower you to navigate the ups and downs of life with strength and determination. Resilience refers to the ability to bounce back from adversity, while perseverance is the steadfast commitment to achieving goals despite obstacles.

These qualities are not innate but can be developed and nurtured through various strategies and mindset shifts. While it's completely normal to feel annoyed or upset at something life has thrown you, the ability to keep going is what will help you develop that inner titan mindset.

- **Embrace a growth mindset:** Embrace the belief that challenges are opportunities for growth and learning rather than insurmountable barriers. By viewing setbacks as opportunities, you can cultivate a positive outlook and the motivation to keep moving forward.
- **Cultivate self-awareness:** Understanding your emotions, reactions, and coping mechanisms is crucial in building resilience. Practicing self-awareness allows you to recognize your strengths, weaknesses, and triggers, enabling you to respond effectively to challenges and stressors.
- **Establish supportive relationships:** Social support is a powerful resource in building resilience. Surround yourself with a network of family, friends, mentors, or support groups that provide encouragement, empathy, and understanding during difficult times. Sharing experiences with others can lessen the burden of challenges and foster a sense of belonging.
- **Develop coping skills:** Resilience is not about avoiding challenges but learning to cope with them effectively. Developing healthy coping strategies such as problem-solving, mindfulness, relaxation techniques, or seeking professional help can enhance resilience and emotional well-being.
- **Set realistic goals:** Perseverance is strengthened when you set realistic and attainable goals. Break down larger objectives into smaller, manageable steps, celebrating progress at each milestone. This approach not only maintains motivation but also provides a sense of accomplishment along the way.
- **Focus on areas of control:** Recognize that not all aspects of life can be controlled. Instead of dwelling on uncontrollable factors, channel your energy into managing what is within

your control. This shift in focus empowers you to take proactive steps and navigate challenges effectively.

- **Embrace failure as part of success:** Perseverance involves embracing failure as a step toward success. Reframe setbacks as opportunities for learning and growth rather than signs of defeat. By viewing failure as a natural part of the journey, individuals are less likely to be discouraged and more willing to persist.
- **Practice adaptability:** Resilience is enhanced when individuals develop adaptability. Flexibility in the face of changing circumstances enables you to adjust your approach, find alternative solutions, and stay focused on your goals despite unexpected challenges.
- **Maintain a healthy lifestyle:** Physical health and mental well-being are intertwined with resilience and perseverance. Regular exercise, proper nutrition, adequate sleep, and stress management contribute to overall resilience and the ability to cope with challenges.

Building resilience and perseverance is a continuous process that requires intentional effort and practice. With these tips, you can embrace challenges with resilience and determination, emerging stronger and more capable of achieving your goals. That doesn't mean you'll never face a difficult situation in your life, but if/when you do, you'll have the tools to overcome it more effectively.

CHAPTER 5

Cultivating Mental Discipline

Mental discipline refers to the ability to control and train your mind, thoughts, and emotions. It's the ultimate level of control. It involves developing self-awareness, focus, concentration, and resilience.

You might wonder how you're supposed to retrain your brain and control every thought, emotion, and action, but it's actually a lot easier than it sounds. The inner titan mindset will automatically do all of this for you and understanding your goals and having an unwavering desire to achieve them, you're already halfway there.

Focus and concentration are good starting points, and these are vital skills that allow you to direct your attention and energy toward specific tasks, ultimately enhancing productivity and overall performance. Just like physical discipline enhances your physical abilities, mental discipline empowers you to sharpen your cognitive faculties, helping you to avoid distractions and stay on track.

But how?

- **Mindfulness meditation:** Mindfulness meditation is a powerful practice that trains the mind to stay present and attentive. Through focused breathing and non-judgmental awareness of thoughts and sensations, you can develop better control over your wandering mind and reduce distractions.

- **Set clear intentions:** Before beginning a task, set a clear intention about what you want to achieve. This helps create a mental roadmap and primes your mind for sustained focus. Clearly defined objectives provide a sense of purpose and direction.
- **Practice single-tasking:** Multitasking may seem efficient, but it often diminishes the quality of work and increases mental fatigue. Engaging in single-tasking, focusing on one task at a time, allows you to channel your mental energy fully and maintain better concentration.
- **Create a distraction-Free environment:** Minimize external distractions in your workspace. Turn off notifications, close unnecessary tabs on your computer, and create a quiet environment that fosters concentration. A clutter-free space contributes to a clutter-free mind.
- **Time blocking:** Divide your day into specific time blocks dedicated to different tasks. By allocating focused time to each activity, you can immerse yourself fully and avoid being overwhelmed by competing priorities.
- **Redirect your attention:** Challenges and setbacks are inevitable, but mental resilience allows you to bounce back from distractions or lapses in concentration without losing focus on your goals. Accept that distractions may occur, and gently redirect your attention when needed.
- **Engage in regular brain exercises:** Just as physical exercise enhances physical strength, cognitive exercises can boost mental discipline. Puzzles, memory games, and brain teasers challenge your mind and improve focus over time.

- **Practice deep work:** Deep work involves sustained, undisturbed concentration on cognitively demanding tasks. Schedule periods of deep work during your most focused and productive hours to maximize mental discipline.
- **Implement the two-minute rule:** If a task takes less than two minutes to complete, do it immediately. This prevents small tasks from accumulating and disrupting your focus on more significant tasks, thus helping you to cultivate mental discipline.
- **Take regular breaks:** While focus is essential, your mind also needs periodic rest. Schedule short breaks to recharge your mental energy. Stepping away from a task and returning with fresh eyes can enhance focus and problem-solving abilities.
- **Use visualization techniques:** Visualize yourself successfully completing tasks with unwavering focus and concentration. This mental rehearsal primes your brain for actual performance and strengthens your resolve.

By incorporating these techniques into your daily routine, you can strengthen your cognitive abilities, develop mental resilience, and elevate your focus and concentration to new heights. With dedication and perseverance, mental discipline becomes a powerful tool for achieving your goals and unlocking your full potential.

Mindfulness & Meditation Techniques

Mindfulness and meditation are powerful practices that promote a deeper connection with the present moment, reduce stress, and enhance overall well-being. However, they are widely misunderstood.

For sure, cultivating these practices requires patience and consistency, but the benefits they offer are more than worth the effort.

Here are some techniques to help you embrace mindfulness and meditation in your daily life:

- **Start with simple breathing exercises:** Begin by focusing on your breath. Take a few moments each day to sit quietly and observe your breath as it naturally flows in and out. Notice the sensations of each inhale and exhale, anchoring your attention to the present moment.

- **Practice mindful walking:** Engage in mindful walking by paying attention to each step you take. Feel the ground beneath your feet, the movement of your legs, and the shifting of your body weight. This practice can be done indoors or outdoors, providing a meditative experience as you move.

- **Set aside dedicated time:** Designate a specific time each day for meditation and mindfulness practice. Consistency is key in establishing these habits. Start with a few minutes each day and gradually increase the duration as you become more comfortable.

- **Create a quiet space:** Find a quiet and comfortable space where you can practice meditation without distractions. This space can be a corner of a room, a cozy nook, or a dedicated meditation area.

- **Utilize guided meditations:** Guided meditations are helpful for beginners and can be found in various forms, including audio recordings, apps, or videos. They offer step-by-step instructions and guidance, making it easier to stay focused during your practice.

- **Practice body scan meditation:** Focus your attention on different parts of your body, starting from your toes and gradually moving upwards. Observe any sensations or tension, allowing yourself to relax and release any stress.

- **Cultivate non-judgmental awareness:** When practicing mindfulness, you must adopt a non-judgmental attitude toward your thoughts and emotions. Rather than trying to suppress or change them, simply observe them without attaching labels or criticisms.

- **Try mindful eating:** During meals, practice mindful eating by savoring each bite, paying attention to the flavors, textures, and smells. This practice fosters a deeper connection with your food and encourages a slower, more mindful approach to eating.

- **Incorporate mindfulness into daily activities:** Extend mindfulness to your daily routines, such as brushing your teeth, taking a shower, or doing household chores. Engage in these activities with full presence and awareness.

- **Be patient with yourself:** Remember that mindfulness and meditation are skills that develop over time. Be patient and compassionate with yourself, acknowledging that the mind may wander during meditation. Gently bring your focus back to the present moment without judgment.

- **Join a meditation group or class:** Consider joining a meditation group or attending meditation classes. Being part of a supportive community can provide encouragement and motivation to maintain your practice.

Mindfulness and meditation are often overlooked because they can be seen as abstract or intangible practices. Some people even assume they're nothing more than hocus pocus. In our fast-paced society, people tend to prioritize productivity and tangible results over taking the time for self-reflection and inner peace. Also, some may view mindfulness and meditation as religious or spiritual practices, which can deter individuals who do not identify with a particular faith.

However, it is important to recognize the numerous benefits that mindfulness and meditation offer. They have been scientifically proven to reduce stress, improve focus and attention span, enhance emotional well-being, boost creativity, increase self-awareness, promote better sleep quality, and even strengthen the immune system.

Of course, you won't know unless you try. It's really that simple. By allowing the benefits of mindfulness and meditation into your life, you'll quickly see that these practices aren't 'hocus pocus' at all, and instead very useful tools to build confidence and a healthier, more positive outlook on life.

Managing Stress Effectively

We can't deny it: stress is an inevitable part of life, but that doesn't mean you can't try to reduce it as much as possible. Effective stress management and the cultivation of mental resilience can significantly improve your ability to cope and maintain a positive outlook when life is trying to get you down.

While a small amount of stress can be a motivator in life, chronic, long-lasting stress can be extremely dangerous for your health. With that in mind, learning how to overcome stress is important.

Here are some helpful tips to help you manage and reduce stress:

- **Identify the source:** Start by identifying what is causing your stress. Is it work-related, personal relationships, or other factors? Understanding the root cause can help you find effective solutions.

- **Practice relaxation techniques:** Engage in activities that promote relaxation such as deep breathing exercises, meditation, yoga, or taking a warm bath. These techniques can help calm your mind and body.

- **Exercise regularly:** Physical activity releases endorphins which are natural mood boosters. Regular exercise not only improves your physical health but also helps reduce stress levels.
- **Prioritize self-care:** Make sure to take care of yourself by getting enough sleep, eating a balanced diet, and engaging in activities that bring you joy and relaxation.
- **Time management:** Organize your time effectively by creating a schedule or to-do list to prioritize tasks and avoid feeling overwhelmed.
- **Seek support from loved ones:** Reach out to friends or family members who can provide emotional support during stressful times. Talking about your feelings with someone you trust can be very helpful.
- **Set boundaries:** Learn to say no when necessary and set healthy boundaries in both personal and professional relationships to avoid taking on too much responsibility.
- **Practice positive thinking:** Challenge negative thoughts by focusing on positive aspects of situations or practicing gratitude for what you have in life.
- **Take breaks:** Incorporate short breaks throughout your day to relax and recharge instead of continuously pushing yourself without any downtime.
- **Learn to say "no":** Saying yes to everything causes you to be overwhelmed and can lead to burn out. If you can't do something, don't have the time, or you just don't want to, it's fine to say "no!"
- **Seek professional help if needed:** If stress becomes overwhelming or starts affecting your daily life significantly,

consider seeking professional help from a therapist who specializes in stress management techniques.

Remember that everyone's journey is unique when it comes to managing stress; therefore, finding what works best for you may require some trial-and-error experimentation until you discover the strategies that bring you the most relief.

Your inner titan never runs from a challenge, but at the same time, he's very aware of the dangers of stress. It's never a failing or a weakness to admit that you're struggling with something; if anything, it's a strength. Embrace your inner titan by admitting when you need a little help, or you just want to talk. A simple action could be all it takes to free you from the grips of stress.

CHAPTER 6

Let's Get Physical

Physical discipline plays a crucial role in fostering self-discipline, helping you to cultivate the mental strength and focus necessary to achieve your goals and lead a fulfilling life.

While the term "physical discipline" often brings to mind images of rigorous exercise in the gym or strict training, its significance extends beyond physical fitness. In fact, physical discipline encompasses a holistic approach that integrates physical activities, healthy habits, and a mindful lifestyle.

So, no, it doesn't necessarily mean you need to join the gym and go every single day before and after work. It just means that you need to be aware of what your body needs and the healthy routes toward building strength from within.

Being disciplined in your body is important for several reasons:

- **Health and well-being:** Discipline helps you maintain a healthy lifestyle by making good choices regarding nutrition, exercise, and rest. It ensures that you prioritize self-care and take care of your physical health, which is crucial for overall well-being.
- **Mental clarity:** When you are physically disciplined, you establish routines and habits that promote mental clarity.

Regular exercise releases endorphins, which improve mood and cognitive function. Eating nutritious food provides the necessary nutrients for optimal brain function.

- **Productivity:** Discipline allows you to stay focused on your goals and tasks at hand. By maintaining a healthy body through discipline, you have more energy, stamina, and mental sharpness to tackle daily challenges effectively.
- **Self-confidence:** Taking care of your body through discipline can boost self-confidence as it improves physical appearance, strength, and overall fitness levels. Feeling good about yourself physically can positively impact other areas of life as well.
- **Longevity:** Physical discipline contributes to longevity by reducing the risk of chronic diseases such as heart disease or diabetes that may arise from an unhealthy lifestyle.

Overall, being disciplined in your body helps create a positive cycle where physical health supports mental well-being while enhancing productivity and self-confidence—all leading to a happier life!

Establishing a Routine For Exercise, Nutrition, & Rest

Creating a well-rounded routine that encompasses exercise, nutrition, and rest is essential for maintaining optimal physical and mental health. This balanced approach ensures that your body receives the necessary nutrients, engages in regular physical activity, and allows sufficient time for recovery and rejuvenation.

By understanding the significance of each component and how they work together, you can learn to build a sustainable and effective routine that supports your overall well-being.

Exercise

Regular exercise is vital for maintaining a healthy body and mind. It strengthens muscles, improves cardiovascular health, and releases endorphins that boost mood and reduce stress. When establishing an exercise routine, consider the following:

- **Choose activities you enjoy:** Opt for physical activities that you genuinely enjoy, whether it's jogging, swimming, cycling, dancing, or practicing yoga. This increases the likelihood of adhering to the routine long-term.
- **Set realistic goals:** Start with achievable fitness goals and gradually progress as you build stamina and strength. Setting realistic milestones helps maintain motivation and prevents burnout.
- **Include variety:** Incorporate a mix of aerobic exercises, strength training, and flexibility exercises to work different muscle groups and promote overall fitness.
- **Schedule regular workouts:** Aim for at least 150 minutes of moderate-intensity aerobic activity or 75 minutes of vigorous-intensity aerobic activity per week, alongside muscle-strengthening exercises on two or more days.

Nutrition

A well-balanced diet provides the body with essential nutrients for energy, growth, and overall health. When developing a nutrition routine, these pieces of advice will help you:

- **Prioritize whole foods:** Focus on whole foods such as fruits, vegetables, whole grains, lean proteins, and healthy fats. In contrast, minimize processed and sugary foods.
- **Practice portion control:** Be mindful of portion sizes to prevent overeating and maintain a healthy weight.

- **Stay hydrated:** Drink plenty of water throughout the day to stay hydrated and support bodily functions.
- **Plan meals and snacks:** Prepare meals and snacks in advance to avoid unhealthy choices when hunger strikes.
- **Consider nutritional needs:** Take into account your nutritional needs, such as dietary restrictions or specific health conditions, and adjust your diet accordingly.

Rest

Rest and sleep are crucial for allowing the body and mind to recover and recharge. There is a false narrative that sleep is for the weak, but trust me, it's a necessary component of a healthy and strong mind, body, and soul. It's not laziness! A well-structured rest routine should include the following:

- **Aim for adequate sleep:** Strive for 7-9 hours of quality sleep each night to support physical and mental well-being.
- **Establish a bedtime routine:** Create a calming bedtime routine to signal the body that it's time to wind down and prepare for sleep.
- **Limit screen time before bed:** Reduce exposure to electronic devices, as blue light can interfere with sleep quality.
- **Schedule rest days:** Incorporate rest days into your exercise routine to allow muscles to recover and prevent overtraining.
- **Manage stress:** Practice stress-reduction techniques, such as meditation, deep breathing, or spending time in nature, to promote relaxation and restful sleep.

Establishing a routine for exercise, nutrition, and rest requires commitment and consistency. Remember that everyone's needs are unique, so tailor your routine to suit your lifestyle, preferences, and health goals.

By taking a holistic approach and integrating these three pillars of well-being, you can create a foundation for a healthier and more balanced life. Your inner titan thrives when your body is strong and healthy.

Enhancing Physical Well-being to Support Self-Discipline

Physical well-being is an integral component of self-discipline, as a healthy body provides the foundation for mental clarity, focus, and overall well-being. Nurturing physical health enables you to strengthen your self-discipline, empowering you to stay on track with your goals and lead a more fulfilling life.

Here are some informative and educational techniques to enhance physical well-being in support of self-discipline:

- **Manage stress:** We already know that chronic stress can take a toll on physical health and self-discipline. To combat that, implement stress-management techniques such as meditation, deep breathing exercises, yoga, or spending time in nature to reduce stress levels and promote a sense of calm.
- **Incorporate mindful movement:** Mindful movement practices such as yoga, tai chi, or qigong can enhance physical flexibility, balance, and mindfulness. These practices not only benefit physical well-being but also cultivate mental discipline and presence.
- **Schedule regular health check-ups:** Regular health check-ups and screenings are essential for early detection of potential health issues. Prioritizing preventive healthcare allows individuals to address any health concerns promptly and maintain their physical well-being. Maybe it's time to make an appointment at the doctor's office?

- **Take regular breaks:** Incorporate short breaks throughout the day to rest your mind and body. Taking breaks from work or mentally demanding tasks can help you recharge and improve focus when you resume your activities. Ironically, this will also help you get more done in the time you have.

- **Develop posture awareness:** Maintain good posture while sitting and standing to prevent musculoskeletal issues and promote overall physical well-being. Pay attention to ergonomics and make necessary adjustments to your workspace. No slouching allowed!

- **Limit sedentary behavior:** Prolonged periods of sedentary behavior can negatively impact physical health. Incorporate movement breaks throughout the day, stand up and stretch, or take short walks to promote circulation and reduce sedentary time. This doesn't mean you have to be 'on the go' all the time but try to break up periods of sitting with at least some movement.

- **Emphasize recovery and rest:** Balance intense physical activity with adequate recovery and rest. Allow your muscles time to recover after strenuous workouts and prioritize restorative activities such as stretching or gentle exercises.

A healthy body provides the energy, focus, and resilience needed to stay on track with goals and maintain a disciplined approach to life's challenges. Remember that physical well-being is a continuous journey that requires consistent effort and commitment, but the rewards for your overall health and self-discipline are undoubtedly worth it.

CHAPTER 7

The Power of Emotional Intelligence & Support Networks

You've no doubt heard of IQ, a measure of your intelligence, but what about EQ? Nothing to do with smarts at all, EQ stands for emotional intelligence and it's something you need to harness and build to allow your inner titan to shine.

Emotions can be extremely powerful, and they have the ability to influence our thoughts, behaviors, and interactions with others. If you don't learn to control your emotions, they will easily control you instead.

When you learn to understand, label, and control your emotions, you have a much better chance of dealing with whatever challenges life throws your way. All of this creates increased emotional intelligence and the ability to avoid 'in the moment' decisions that could later turn out to be negative.

Let's check out some of the major benefits of developing emotional intelligence, so you can understand just how vital it is:

- **Improved self-awareness:** Emotional intelligence helps you understand your emotions, strengths, weaknesses, and values. This self-awareness allows you to make better decisions and navigate challenging situations with greater ease.

- **Effective communication:** People with high emotional intelligence are skilled at expressing their thoughts and feelings in a clear and empathetic manner. They also have a better understanding of non-verbal cues, making them more effective communicators.
- **Enhanced empathy:** Emotional intelligence enables you to understand and share the feelings of others. This ability fosters stronger relationships by allowing you to connect on a deeper level with friends, family members, colleagues, or even strangers.
- **Conflict resolution:** Those with high emotional intelligence excel at managing conflicts by remaining calm under pressure and finding mutually beneficial solutions. They can effectively navigate disagreements while maintaining positive relationships.
- **Leadership skills:** Leaders who possess emotional intelligence inspire trust among their team members through active listening, empathy, and understanding individual motivations. Such leaders create an inclusive work environment that promotes collaboration and productivity.
- **Stress management:** Emotional intelligence equips you with effective strategies for managing stress levels in both personal and professional settings. By recognizing your emotions during stressful situations, you can respond in a more constructive manner.
- **Adaptability:** People with high emotional intelligence are adaptable to change because they possess the ability to regulate their emotions effectively when faced with unexpected circumstances or challenges.
- **Positive mental health:** Emotional intelligence is closely linked to improved mental well-being as it helps you develop resilience against negative emotions such as anxiety or depression by fostering healthier coping mechanisms.

While there isn't a number scale to measure emotional intelligence, it's something you'll just know you have. You'll feel calmer in yourself, and you won't second guess every single decision and interaction you have with people. It will allow you to simply observe situations and give it a moment before making a decision, rather than jumping in feet first and perhaps making the wrong choice you'll regret later.

So, how can you get started with building your EQ? Here are some informative strategies:

- **Recognize and identify motions:** The first step in managing emotions is recognizing and identifying them accurately. Take the time to understand what you are feeling and why you might be experiencing those emotions. Name the emotions you are experiencing to gain clarity and prevent them from overwhelming you.
- **Practice mindfulness:** Mindfulness techniques, such as meditation and deep breathing, help create a sense of present-moment awareness. Mindfulness allows you to observe your emotions without judgment, providing a more objective perspective on your emotional experiences.
- **Develop emotional awareness:** Cultivate emotional awareness by paying attention to physical cues associated with various emotions. Recognize how different emotions manifest in your body, such as increased heart rate for anxiety or a feeling of warmth for happiness. Understanding these physical indicators helps manage emotions effectively.
- **Use cognitive restructuring:** Challenge and reframe negative or irrational thoughts that contribute to intense emotions. Replace unhelpful thoughts with more balanced and constructive ones. Cognitive restructuring helps you gain control over your emotional responses and prevents unnecessary distress.

- **Engage in physical activity:** Physical exercise is a powerful tool for regulating emotions. Engaging in activities like walking, jogging, or yoga releases endorphins, which are natural mood-boosters to reduce stress and anxiety.

- **Seek social support:** Talk to friends, family, or a therapist about your emotions and experiences. Sharing feelings with others can provide validation and perspective, helping to manage emotions more effectively.

- **Create a safe space:** Designate a physical space where you can retreat when overwhelmed by emotions. This space can serve as a calming environment for reflection and relaxation.

- **Practice deep breathing:** Deep breathing exercises activate the body's relaxation response, which can counteract the physiological effects of stress and intense emotions.

- **Use relaxation techniques:** Incorporate relaxation techniques, such as progressive muscle relaxation or guided imagery, into your routine to manage stress and emotional intensity.

- **Implement time-outs:** When emotions become overwhelming, take a time-out to step away from the situation temporarily. This break allows you to collect your thoughts and emotions before responding more calmly.

- **Journal your emotions:** Keep a journal to express and process your emotions. Writing about your feelings can provide clarity and insight into their triggers, making it easier to manage them effectively.

- **Practice self-compassion:** Be kind to yourself during challenging times. Recognize that everyone experiences a range of emotions, and it's okay to have emotional ups and downs. Practice self-compassion and treat yourself with understanding and care.

Building Healthy Relationships & Effective Communication Skills

Healthy relationships and effective communication skills are essential components of personal and professional success. Without them, you'll struggle to get your point across, fail to interact positively with others, and all of this leads to frustration and misunderstandings. On the other hand, nurturing positive connections with others not only fosters emotional well-being but also leads to collaboration, mutual understanding, and conflict resolution.

By cultivating strong communication skills, you can express yourself clearly, listen actively, and build meaningful relationships.

These techniques will help you build healthy relationships and develop effective communication skills:

- **Active listening:** Listening actively involves giving your full attention to the speaker and genuinely seeking to understand their perspective. Practice active listening by maintaining eye contact, nodding to show understanding, and providing verbal cues, such as "I see" or "I understand." Once they've finished talking, you can also briefly summarize the main points of what they've said, to show them that you've taken it all on board.

- **Empathy and understanding:** Empathy is the ability to put yourself in someone else's shoes and comprehend their feelings and experiences. Show empathy by acknowledging their emotions and validating their experiences, even if you don't necessarily agree with their point of view. Keep an open mind and try to imagine how you would feel if you were in that person's situation. Practicing this regularly will help you to build empathy for those around you.

- **Assertiveness:** Being assertive means expressing your thoughts, needs, and boundaries respectfully and directly. Practice assertive communication by using "I" statements to express your feelings and avoid aggressive or passive-aggressive behaviors. It may feel awkward at first, but standing tall, maintaining open body language (not slouching or avoiding eye contact), and feeling confident enough to say "no" when you need to, all contributes.

- **Non-verbal communication:** Non-verbal cues, such as facial expressions, gestures, and body language, play a significant role in communication. Pay attention to your own non-verbal cues and be attuned to those of others to better understand the underlying messages being conveyed. For instance, avoiding eye contact can mean that somebody is lying, but it can also mean that they're nervous. The rest of their body language will help you decipher the puzzle. Avoid crossing your arms over your body when you're talking to someone, as this shows defensiveness. Instead, keep your hands by your sides or loosely in your lap if you're sitting. Nod along when they're speaking and maintain eye contact. Avoid fidgeting, as this makes you look uninterested or bored.

- **Open-mindedness:** Approach conversations with an open mind, being receptive to different perspectives and ideas. Avoid jumping to conclusions or making assumptions and be willing to explore alternative viewpoints. Just listen, take everything on board, and analyze their points from a place of neutrality.

- **Conflict resolution:** Conflict is a natural part of relationships, but effective communication can help resolve conflicts constructively and avoid major issues. Focus on the specific issue at hand, listen to the other person's concerns, and work together to find a mutually satisfactory solution. If you need to leave the room for five minutes to calm down, do so. This will help you avoid behaviors driven by anger; deep breathing can help ground you in these difficult moments.

- **Managing emotions:** Emotional regulation is crucial during communication. Avoid reacting impulsively to emotions and take time to process your feelings before responding. Communicate calmly and respectfully, even during challenging discussions. When you notice you're feeling a specific emotion, give yourself a second to name it. Then, take a moment to calm down before you go back to the situation.
- **Feedback and constructive criticism:** Offering feedback and constructive criticism in a supportive manner helps build trust and fosters personal growth. Provide specific examples and focus on behaviors rather than personal attributes when offering feedback. Also be mindful of the language you use; avoid blame-words, such as, "You always..." or "You make me feel..." Instead, say things like, "I feel sad when you ..." or "I can see that you're struggling, can I help?" This takes the blame away and keeps things neutral.
- **Avoiding negative communication patterns:** Be mindful of negative communication patterns, such as blame, defensiveness, or stonewalling. Instead, strive for open and honest communication that fosters understanding and cooperation. This takes some self-reflection as you'll need to identify the types of behaviors you have a tendency toward. A journal can help you here, but once you unravel the puzzle, focus on overcoming those patterns and replacing them with healthier, more positive routes forward.
- **Flexibility and adaptability:** Be willing to adapt your communication style to accommodate different personalities and situations. Being flexible in your approach can lead to more effective interactions and stronger relationships.
- **Expressing gratitude and appreciation:** Regularly express gratitude and appreciation to those you interact with. Recognizing and acknowledging others' contributions

and efforts can strengthen the bond and create a positive communication environment.

- **Learning from others:** Observe effective communicators and learn from their techniques. Take note of how they actively listen, show empathy, and handle challenging conversations. Incorporate these learnings into your own communication style.

Building healthy relationships and developing effective communication skills is an ongoing process that requires practice and self-awareness. Remember that communication is a two-way process, and actively working on improving your communication skills can lead to more enriching and fulfilling relationships. It will also open many doors for you in terms of your career and personal success.

Building a Supportive Environment

Self-discipline is the cornerstone of personal growth and achievement. Without it, you'll just end up being blown off course by the tiniest breeze. It empowers you to stay focused, overcome challenges, and work diligently toward your goals. However, it is essential to recognize that self-discipline is not solely a product of individual willpower; there is more to discover here.

The environment in which you live, work, and interact plays a significant role in shaping and influencing your level of self-discipline. The right environment can work wonders, but the wrong one can completely derail your efforts and lead you to give up.

The physical environment includes your home, workplace, and the places you frequent, while the social environment involves the people you interact with regularly, such as family, friends, and colleagues. Each of these elements has a direct or indirect influence on your self-discipline.

For instance, a cluttered and chaotic physical environment can lead to distractions and reduce focus, hindering self-discipline. It's true that a tidy desk means a tidy mind, and that goes beyond the office setting. A well-organized and conducive setting can foster concentration and reinforce disciplined habits. Put simply, it gets you in the right head space to do what you need to do and avoid procrastination.

However, social interactions can be equally influential. Surrounding yourself with supportive and disciplined individuals can positively impact your own self-discipline. On the other hand, spending time with individuals who lack self-discipline might lead to adopting similar behaviors, as these negative elements have a habit of becoming contagious.

The Role of Habits

Habits play a crucial role in self-discipline, and your environment is a key factor in habit formation and maintenance. Habits are developed through repetition and reinforcement, and the environment can facilitate or obstruct this process.

For instance, an environment that encourages positive habits, such as a gym or a quiet study area, can make it easier to stick to disciplined routines. But an environment filled with temptations or distractions, like an area with unhealthy food options or constant interruptions, can challenge your ability to maintain self-discipline. So, perhaps it's time to tidy out your kitchen cupboards?

The Effect of Accountability

Accountability is important for self-discipline because it helps to keep you focused, motivated, and on track toward your goals. When you are accountable to someone or something, you feel a sense of responsibility to follow through on your commitments. This motivation can help you stay disciplined even when faced with challenges or temptations.

In addition, accountability provides structure and consistency in your actions. Knowing that you have someone holding you accountable can prevent procrastination and encourage you to consistently work toward your goals.

Of course, it also means having someone who can provide feedback, guidance, and support along the way. This external perspective can help you identify areas for improvement, celebrate successes, and overcome obstacles.

Joining a supportive group or having an accountability partner who shares similar goals can provide motivation and encouragement. Participating in an environment that recognizes and rewards disciplined behavior can reinforce and sustain self-discipline too.

Strategies for Creating a Supportive & Empowering Social Circle

The power of your social circle should not be underestimated. The people you surround yourself with can profoundly influence your emotions, behaviors, and overall well-being. Building a supportive and empowering social circle is essential for personal growth, motivation, and success.

But how can you make sure that you're building and nurturing the right kind of social circle to help propel you toward success and overall happiness?

- **Define your values and goals:** Before you do anything, take the time to define your core values and long-term goals. Knowing what you stand for and what you aim to achieve will help you attract like-minded individuals who share your vision. Seek those who align with your values and can contribute positively to your journey.
- **Be open and approachable:** Creating an empowering social circle starts with being open to new connections and

experiences. Approach social situations with an open mind and a friendly demeanor. Engage in conversations and show genuine interest in others' perspectives and aspirations. Being approachable will make it easier for like-minded individuals to gravitate toward you.

- **Join groups and communities:** Find groups, organizations, or communities that align with your interests and passions. Whether it's a hobby club, a professional association, or a volunteer group, participating in such gatherings provides an excellent opportunity to meet people with shared interests. Common interests serve as a strong foundation for nurturing supportive relationships.
- **Be supportive and encouraging:** Being supportive and encouraging towards others is a key factor in building an empowering social circle. Show genuine care and empathy, celebrate their successes, and offer a helping hand during challenging times. When you are supportive, others are more likely to reciprocate, fostering an atmosphere of empowerment and trust within the group.
- **Weed out toxic relationships:** Unfortunately, we all have that one person, or perhaps more than one person, who drags us down and offers nothing positive to our lives. It's sad to realize it, but as you seek to create an empowering social circle, it is essential to identify and distance yourself from toxic relationships. Negative and unsupportive individuals can drain your energy and hinder personal growth, not to mention affect your overall happiness and well-being. Recognize the impact of such relationships on your well-being and take necessary steps to distance yourself from them, making room for more positive connections.
- **Attend personal development events:** Participate in personal development workshops, seminars, or conferences. These

events provide opportunities to meet like-minded individuals who are actively seeking growth and improvement in their lives. Engaging in such gatherings can lead to meaningful connections with people who share a commitment to personal empowerment.

- **Embrace diversity:** An empowering social circle can be enriched by diversity in perspectives, backgrounds, and experiences. Embrace the differences in others and be open to learning from their unique viewpoints. Diversity can lead to personal growth, expanding your horizons and broadening your understanding of the world. It's a great way to avoid the echo chamber, where collaborating with those around you simply leads to the same limited ideas; diversity will show you that the world is much larger and more complex than you could ever imagine, packed with opportunities to explore.
- **Engage in mutual growth:** A truly empowering social circle encourages mutual growth and support. Engage in activities that foster learning and development together. This could include reading and discussing books, attending workshops as a group, or setting and pursuing collective goals. Such shared experiences strengthen the bond within the circle and contribute to each member's personal growth journey.

The right people in your life can help build you up, or they can aid in knocking you down. It's never easy to realize that you may have people in your life whose intentions aren't as pure as you might think. But it's never a loss because moving away from them simply makes room for people who offer light and positivity.

Take the time to examine the social circle you currently have and ask whether it's time to expand your horizons a little. Who knows who is out there, just waiting for you to arrive?

Optimizing Physical Spaces For Productivity & Discipline

We know that the environment in which you work and live plays a significant role in shaping your productivity and discipline. A well-organized and purposefully designed physical space can enhance focus, boost motivation, and cultivate a disciplined mindset.

Begin by decluttering your physical space, removing unnecessary items, and organizing essential materials. A clean and tidy environment promotes mental clarity, enabling you to focus better on tasks and goals.

Here are a few tips to help you create that ideal space to live, work, and play:

- **A dedicated workspace:** Creating a designated workspace, whether at home or in an office, is crucial for establishing a productive and disciplined routine. A separate workspace helps mentally compartmentalize work from leisure, minimizing distractions and improving concentration during work hours.
- **Ergonomic considerations:** Physical comfort is vital for maintaining focus and discipline throughout extended periods of work. Invest in ergonomic furniture and accessories, such as an adjustable chair, a properly positioned monitor, and a supportive keyboard. Ergonomic setups reduce physical strain, allowing you to stay focused and productive for more extended periods.
- **Optimize lighting:** Proper lighting is a powerful tool for boosting productivity and discipline. Natural light is preferable, as it enhances mood and alertness. Position your workspace near a window to benefit from daylight. When natural light is limited, use warm and adjustable artificial lighting to create a pleasant and well-lit atmosphere.

- **Incorporate greenery:** Introducing plants and greenery into your workspace can have a surprisingly positive impact on productivity and discipline. Plants not only improve air quality but also add a touch of nature, which can reduce stress and enhance creativity.

- **Minimize distractions:** Identify and minimize potential distractions in your physical space. Keep mobile devices on silent or out of sight during focused work hours. If possible, create a space away from high-traffic areas or noisy environments to maintain concentration.

- **Personalize your space:** Personalizing your workspace can foster a sense of ownership and motivation. Display motivational quotes, pictures of loved ones, or items that represent your goals and aspirations. These personal touches can serve as reminders of what you are working towards, reinforcing discipline and determination.

- **Utilize productivity tools:** Incorporate productivity tools and organization systems into your physical space. Whiteboards, calendars, and task management software can help you plan and track progress effectively. Visualizing your goals and deadlines can encourage self-discipline and time management.

- **Implement break areas:** Discipline is not solely about constant work; it also involves taking intentional breaks to recharge. Create designated break areas where you can step away from work briefly, stretch, or engage in relaxation exercises. Scheduled breaks can prevent burnout and maintain focus when you return to work.

A well-designed physical space can be the catalyst for unlocking your full potential and achieving remarkable results. You don't have to go in there and completely overhaul your house, but making a few, select changes could make all the difference.

CHAPTER 8

Sustaining Long-Term Self-Discipline

You've learned a lot about self-discipline so far, and by this point, you know that it is a fundamental trait that enables you to stay focused, motivated, and consistent in pursuing your goals. The challenge comes when trying to maintain that level of discipline over a long period of time.

Of course, life will throw you curveballs and you'll go through periods of joy and sadness: that's just life. But implementing certain strategies can significantly enhance your ability to stay on track and achieve long-term success.

- **Set clear and meaningful goals**: The foundation of self-discipline lies in having well-defined and purposeful goals. Remember to make sure they are specific, measurable, achievable, relevant, and time-bound (SMART). Additionally, connect these goals to your broader life vision, values, and passions.
- **Develop a consistent routine**: Establishing a structured daily routine can work wonders for maintaining self-discipline. A consistent schedule not only creates a sense of order but also eliminates decision fatigue by automating mundane tasks. Allocate specific time blocks for work, exercise, leisure, and personal development. Stick to this routine as much as

possible, even during weekends or holidays, as it reinforces discipline and strengthens self-control.

- **Prioritize time management**: Time is a finite resource, and managing it effectively is critical to long-term self-discipline. Use time management techniques and avoid time-wasting activities like excessive social media browsing or procrastination. Instead, allocate more time to pursuits that align with your goals.
- **Cultivate self-awareness**: Being self-aware allows you to recognize your strengths, weaknesses, triggers, and limitations. As tough as it can be, acknowledge any tendencies towards procrastination or self-sabotage. Regularly assess your progress, celebrate achievements, and learn from setbacks. The more you understand yourself, the better you can tailor your strategies for maintaining self-discipline.
- **Create a distraction-free environment**: Minimize distractions in your physical and digital environment to help maintain concentration. Designate a dedicated workspace that promotes productivity and remove any potential temptations or interruptions. It's a good idea to consider using website blockers during work hours or keeping your phone on silent mode to avoid unnecessary distractions.
- **Practice mindfulness and meditation:** Mindfulness practices, such as meditation, can improve your focus, reduce stress, and enhance self-discipline. Regular meditation sessions can train your mind to remain present and control impulses. Moreover, mindfulness helps you become more conscious of your thoughts and emotions, enabling you to respond to challenges calmly and rationally.
- **Build habits gradually**: Developing new habits is crucial for long-term self-discipline, but trying to adopt too many changes simultaneously can lead to burnout and failure.

Instead, focus on building one or two habits at a time. Start small and gradually increase the difficulty or complexity of your habits over time. Consistent, incremental progress is more sustainable than attempting drastic transformations, and a whole less stressful too.

- **Surround yourself with supportive individuals**: Remember, the people you surround yourself with can significantly influence your self-discipline. Seek out individuals who share your goals or possess strong self-discipline themselves. Engaging with supportive and like-minded individuals can provide encouragement, accountability, and valuable insights to keep you on track.
- **Reward yourself appropriately**: Rewarding yourself for achieving milestones or staying disciplined can reinforce positive behavior. However, it's essential to choose rewards that align with your goals and are not counterproductive. For instance, if your aim is to maintain a healthy diet, treating yourself to a high-calorie dessert might undermine your efforts.
- **Embrace failure as a learning opportunity**: Nobody is perfect, and setbacks are a natural part of the journey towards self-discipline. Instead of being disheartened by failure, view it as an opportunity to learn and grow. Analyze what went wrong, identify areas for improvement, and use that knowledge to refine your strategies for the future.

Maintaining self-discipline over the long term requires consistent effort and dedication. It may seem like a long road, but remember that self-discipline is a skill that can be developed and strengthened with practice, and every small step forward contributes to long-term success.

Techniques for Self-Monitoring & Tracking Progress

Self-monitoring and progress tracking are essential aspects of personal development and goal achievement. By observing your behaviors and measuring your progress, you gain valuable insights into your strengths, weaknesses, and areas for improvement. It also helps you spot problems that might stop you from moving forward, and then you can take action before the issue becomes too ingrained.

Let's explore various techniques for self-monitoring and tracking progress that can help you stay focused, motivated, and accountable on your journey toward success:

- **Daily journals and reflection**: Keeping a daily journal allows you to record your thoughts, actions, and emotions. This reflective practice provides a deeper understanding of patterns, triggers, and behaviors that may impact self-discipline and progress towards goals. Regularly reviewing journal entries helps identify areas that need improvement and encourages self-awareness.
- **Goal setting and action plans**: Setting goals provides a clear roadmap for tracking progress. Break down long-term goals into smaller milestones and create action plans to achieve each one. Regularly assess your progress against these milestones to maintain focus and celebrate achievements.
- **Habit trackers**: Habit trackers are tools that help you monitor your daily routines and habits. These trackers can be physical notebooks, smartphone apps, or digital spreadsheets. Consistently tracking habits, such as exercise, reading, or meditation, helps you to recognize patterns and stay committed to positive behaviors.
- **Time management techniques**: Effective time management is crucial for tracking progress and maintaining self-discipline.

Use techniques like the Pomodoro Technique, time blocking, or the Eisenhower Matrix to prioritize tasks and allocate time efficiently. These methods help prevent procrastination and maintain productivity throughout the day.

- **Data visualization:** Visualizing data can be a powerful motivator for self-monitoring and progress tracking. Create charts, graphs, or progress bars to represent your achievements visually. Seeing the growth and improvement over time can boost motivation and reinforce self-discipline.
- **Peer or mentor feedback:** Seeking feedback from peers or mentors provides an external perspective on your progress and performance. Constructive criticism and encouragement from others can offer valuable insights, helping you identify blind spots and areas where adjustments may be necessary.
- **Utilizing mobile apps and technology:** Numerous mobile apps and technology platforms are designed to assist with self-monitoring and tracking progress. From fitness apps to habit trackers and goal-setting platforms, these tools make it convenient to record and analyze data, providing real-time feedback on your journey.
- **Self-assessment and personal checklists:** Regularly assessing your skills, knowledge, and achievements allows you to gauge your progress objectively. Create self-assessment checklists to evaluate your strengths and areas for improvement. Honest self-evaluation fosters a growth mindset and encourages ongoing development.
- **Accountability partners or support groups:** Engaging with accountability partners or joining support groups fosters a sense of responsibility and encouragement. Regular check-ins with these individuals or groups can motivate you to stay on track, offer support during challenges, and celebrate achievements together.

Remember, tracking progress is not just about recording achievements; it is also about recognizing areas for improvement and maintaining accountability on your path to success.

Dealing With Plateaus, Complacency, & Maintaining Motivation

When you're on any self-development journey, it's normal to encounter plateaus and periods of complacency that can hinder progress. These plateaus, characterized by a lack of noticeable improvement or stagnation, can be demotivating, and challenging to overcome. However, with the right strategies and mindset, it is possible to navigate these obstacles and maintain motivation to continue pushing forward, just like your inner titan wants.

- **Recognize plateaus as natural**: The first step in dealing with plateaus is acknowledging that they are a natural part of any growth process. Almost every endeavor, whether it's learning a new skill, pursuing a career, or achieving fitness goals, will encounter periods of slow progress or leveling off. Understanding this can help you avoid unnecessary frustration and disappointment.

- **Reframe your perspective**: Rather than viewing plateaus as setbacks, see them as opportunities for learning and reinforcement. Plateaus provide a chance to solidify the skills or knowledge you've acquired so far. Embrace these phases as a time to refine your techniques, review your strategies, and focus on mastery.

- **Set specific milestones**: Breaking your long-term goals into smaller, achievable milestones can help you track your progress more effectively. When you hit a plateau, celebrate the milestones you've reached, and use them as evidence of your overall advancement. Celebrating small victories can reignite your motivation and spur you on to tackle the next set of challenges.

- **Embrace continuous learning**: One of the best ways to overcome plateaus and avoid complacency is to maintain a mindset of continuous learning. Seek out new knowledge, take courses, attend workshops, or engage in self-study to expand your skills and understanding. A commitment to lifelong learning keeps your mind active and motivated.

- **Step outside your comfort zone:** Complacency often arises from staying within your comfort zone for too long. To break free from this stagnation, challenge yourself with new and more demanding tasks. Pushing beyond your current limits can reignite your motivation, create new opportunities for growth, and foster a sense of accomplishment.

- **Find inspiration and role models**: Surround yourself with inspiring individuals who have achieved what you aspire to accomplish. Learn from their journeys, struggles, and triumphs. Hearing about the challenges they faced and how they overcame them can serve as a powerful motivator during your own challenging times.

- **Reevaluate and adjust goals**: Periodically reassess your long-term goals and consider whether they remain relevant and meaningful. It's possible that circumstances or priorities have changed, and adjusting your goals accordingly can provide a fresh sense of purpose and direction. Be flexible in your approach and willing to adapt as needed.

- **Focus on the process, not just the outcome**: While having clear goals is essential, concentrating solely on the end result can be overwhelming, especially during plateaus. Shift your focus to the process of growth and improvement. Remember to celebrate the effort you put in, the skills you develop, and the knowledge you gain along the way. You deserve a pat on the back!

- **Seek support and accountability**: Share your journey with friends, family, or like-minded individuals who can offer support and encouragement. Establishing an accountability system can be particularly helpful during complacent phases and tough times. Regular check-ins or progress reports with someone you trust can motivate you to stay committed to your goals.
- **Practice positive self-talk**: Maintain a positive and encouraging inner dialogue. Avoid self-criticism during plateaus, as it can erode self-confidence and motivation. Instead, remind yourself of past achievements, reflect on the progress you've made, and maintain belief in your ability to overcome challenges. Regularly check in with yourself to recognize negative self-talk; once you notice it, reframe what you're telling yourself and repeat consistently.

Dealing with plateaus, complacency, and maintaining motivation are integral aspects of personal and professional growth. Everyone deals with these frustrating roadblocks but overcoming them is easier than it seems. Remember that maintaining motivation is an ongoing process, and it requires consistent effort and a growth-oriented mindset to overcome obstacles and continue progressing toward your goals.

Celebrating Milestones & Practicing Self-Reward

Now comes the fun part!

Achieving goals and making progress toward your aspirations is a significant part of personal growth and success. Celebrating milestones along the way and practicing self-reward are essential components of maintaining motivation and fostering a positive mindset.

It's easy to become so focused on the end result that you forget to appreciate the progress you make along the way. Recognizing and acknowledging even the smallest steps forward is vital for several reasons:

- **Motivation boost:** Celebrating milestones provides an immediate boost to your motivation. When you acknowledge your progress, you reinforce the belief that you are capable of achieving your goals, and this sense of accomplishment fuels your determination to keep going.
- **Positive reinforcement:** Celebrating milestones acts as positive reinforcement for the effort and hard work you invest in your pursuits. It helps create a positive feedback loop, making you more likely to continue putting in the necessary effort to reach your next milestone.
- **Stress reduction:** Acknowledging progress helps to combat stress and burnout. By taking time to celebrate your achievements, you allow yourself to relax and rejuvenate, preventing feelings of overwhelm and exhaustion.
- **Sustaining momentum:** Recognizing milestones helps you maintain momentum on your journey. It reminds you of how far you've come and encourages you to stay committed to your goals, even during challenging times.
- **Increased happiness:** Celebrations trigger the release of endorphins, neurotransmitters responsible for feelings of happiness and pleasure. Embracing this joy reinforces your positive association with your goals and encourages you to persist.
- **Strengthened resilience:** Celebrating milestones builds resilience by providing a reminder of your ability to overcome obstacles and succeed. This fortifies your determination to face future challenges with confidence.

- **Enhanced self-confidence:** Recognizing your progress enhances self-confidence and self-esteem. When you appreciate your efforts and accomplishments, you develop a stronger belief in your capabilities.

- **Improved focus:** Celebrating milestones allows you to pause and reflect on your journey. This reflection aids in clarifying your objectives, making necessary adjustments, and sharpening your focus on the next steps.

Practicing Self-Reward Effectively

Self-reward is an integral part of celebrating milestones. But how can you reward yourself in a healthy and effective way?

- **Set milestone rewards:** Before embarking on your journey, establish a reward system tied to specific milestones, i.e., when those rewards are going to take place. These rewards can range from small treats for minor achievements to more significant rewards for major milestones. Align the rewards with activities or items that bring you joy and reinforce positive behavior.

- **Personalize the celebration:** Tailor the celebration to your preferences and interests. It could be indulging in a hobby, spending time with loved ones, or taking a break to enjoy some well-deserved relaxation. It needs to be something you enjoy, making it worth working toward.

- **Express gratitude:** Express gratitude towards yourself for the hard work and dedication you've put into your endeavors. Acknowledge the progress with a positive mindset and appreciate the learning experiences gained along the way.

- **Capture the moment:** Document your milestones and celebrations through journaling, photographs, or videos. This creates a tangible record of your progress, which you can refer back to during challenging times.

- **Share your success:** Share your achievements and celebrations with friends, family, or a supportive community. Not only does this reinforce your sense of accomplishment, but it also allows others to share in your joy and provide encouragement.

Celebrating milestones and practicing self-reward are crucial components of a successful and fulfilling journey toward your goals. Unleashing your inner titan isn't only about hard work and perseverance; it's also about fun and enjoyment along the way.

Remember to appreciate the journey as much as the destination and cherish each milestone as a stepping stone toward even greater accomplishments.

CHAPTER 9

Conquering Self-Doubt & Building Confidence

We live in a world of constant criticism and the need to prove ourselves. It's exhausting, I'm sure you'll agree. But within all of that, confidence can help you overcome the barrage of negativity.

The first thing you need to overcome is self-doubt. It's as prevalent as rain in the winter, but it's not helpful in the slightest. Self-doubt is the feeling of uncertainty or lack of confidence in yourself or your abilities. It often involves questioning your decisions, skills, or worthiness.

Self-doubt can arise from various factors such as past failures, comparison to others, fear of judgment, or a lack of validation. However, it is important to remember that self-doubt is a common experience and something that can be overcome with self-reflection, support from others, and building self-confidence. That's exactly what we're going to explore in this chapter.

Believe it or not, everyone experiences self-doubt from time to time, even the most confident of people. It's a natural human emotion that can affect anyone in various aspects of life, including personal relationships, career, and self-development. While occasional self-doubt is normal, allowing it to persist and dictate your actions can hinder personal growth and lead to missed opportunities.

To help you side-step these troubling effects, let's explore the signs of self-doubt, its impact, and effective strategies to recognize and overcome it, ultimately building confidence and resilience. Your inner titan will remain shackled unless you overcome this important challenge.

Recognizing Self-Doubt

These signs indicate that you're dealing with self-doubt:

- **Negative self-talk:** Constantly engaging in negative self-talk, such as doubting your capabilities, criticizing your decisions, or expecting failure, is a clear sign of self-doubt. It's that little voice in the back of your head that says you can't do something, or you're bad at a particular task.
- **Fear of failure:** A strong fear of failure, often leading to avoidance of challenges or new experiences, can be rooted in self-doubt and a lack of confidence in your abilities. This can stop you from going out there and getting what you really want.
- **Seeking constant validation:** Relying excessively on external validation or seeking approval from others before making decisions may indicate a lack of self-trust and self-doubt. You don't need anyone else's approval as long as whatever you're doing sits well with you.
- **Downplaying achievements:** Minimizing your achievements or attributing them to luck or external factors rather than acknowledging your skills and efforts is a manifestation of self-doubt. If you achieve something, it's because you're good at it and you put in the hard work.

- **Comparing yourself to others:** Constantly comparing yourself to others and feeling inadequate or inferior can be a clear indication of self-doubt. This issue is extremely prevalent these days because of social media. We see everyone else having a seemingly amazing time and it makes us doubt our appearance, achievements, and progress in life.

Let's dwell on the last point for a second longer, since it's extremely important and very common these days.

Comparing yourself to others can be dangerous for several reasons. Firstly, it can lead to a negative self-image and low self-esteem. When you constantly compare yourself to others, you may focus on their strengths and achievements while disregarding your own unique qualities and accomplishments. This can create feelings of inadequacy and dissatisfaction within yourself. The truth is that you're more than worthy; you simply need to open your eyes to see it.

Secondly, comparing yourself to others often involves making unfair comparisons. Each person has their own journey, experiences, and circumstances that shape who they are and what they have achieved. It is not a fair or accurate measure of your worth or success to compare yourself directly with someone else.

It can also hinder personal growth and development. Instead of focusing on your own progress and goals, you may become preoccupied with trying to match or surpass the achievements of others. This can prevent you from exploring your true potential or pursuing paths that align with your passions and values. You might also find yourself veering totally off course and living someone else's life instead of your own, losing yourself in the process.

Remember, we all have different strengths, talents, perspectives, and life paths that make us special in our own way. Embracing these differences rather than constantly comparing yourself allows for greater self-acceptance and fosters a more positive outlook on life.

Instead of falling into the trap of comparison, it is important to focus on personal growth, celebrate your own successes no matter how small they may seem in comparison with others', and practice gratitude for what you have accomplished so far in life while setting realistic goals for the future based on your own desires rather than external influences.

Your inner titan wants to embrace your path wholeheartedly.

The Impact of Self-Doubt

Aside from comparisons, self-doubt can have significant negative effects on various aspects of life in general. Failing to recognize these effects will simply mean you constantly avoid meeting your potential.

- **Limiting potential:** When you doubt your abilities, you may avoid taking on challenges or pursuing opportunities that could lead to personal and professional growth. It's almost as though you ask, "What's the point?" You don't believe you're good enough to succeed, so you don't try.
- **Undermining confidence:** Persistent self-doubt erodes self-confidence, making it difficult to trust your instincts and make decisive choices. Again, you simply stand still, not taking positive opportunities that come your way.
- **Creating anxiety and stress:** Constantly questioning yourself can lead to increased anxiety and stress, affecting overall well-being and mental health.
- **Hindering relationships:** Self-doubt can impact your interactions with others, leading to difficulties in forming meaningful connections and fostering healthy relationships. If you don't believe you're good enough, how can you expect anyone else to? In this case, you might find yourself veering toward toxic relationships, rather than healthy ones.

Strategies to Overcome Self-Doubt

Recognizing self-doubt is the first step to recovery, but what comes next? You need to actively work toward challenging self-doubt and overcoming the shackles it places on your life.

These strategies will help you overcome obstacles and keep moving forward:

- **Challenge negative thoughts:** Pay attention to your thoughts and challenge negative self-talk. Once you recognize that you're criticizing yourself, stop, and replace self-doubting thoughts with positive and affirming ones that acknowledge your strengths and accomplishments. It will take time and effort to do, but repetition is vital in rewiring your brain to believe what you want it to.
- **Set realistic goals:** Break down your goals into manageable and achievable steps. Celebrate each milestone you reach, reinforcing your belief in your abilities. With each box ticked, look forward to a great leap forward.
- **Embrace failure as a learning opportunity:** Shift your perspective on failure. Instead of seeing it as a reflection of your worth, view it as an opportunity to learn and grow. Analyze what went wrong and use the experience to improve. We all make mistakes and sometimes things don't work out how we want them to, but that doesn't mean we can't find the small chink of light and work with it to change the future.
- **Practice self-compassion:** Treat yourself with the same kindness and understanding that you would offer a friend facing similar challenges. Practice self-compassion by acknowledging that everyone experiences self-doubt at times. After all, we tend to be extremely kind to our loved ones, but very harsh on ourselves. Question why you do that and change the narrative.

- **Limit social media comparisons:** We talked about how harmful this is, and this point is key. Reduce exposure to social media or be mindful of how you engage with it. Comparing yourself to curated portrayals of others on social media can exacerbate self-doubt and simply leaves you feeling 'less than.'

- **Seek support:** Talk to friends, family, or a therapist about your feelings of self-doubt. Sharing your struggles can provide perspective and support, helping you navigate through challenging times.

- **Focus on your strengths:** Identify and focus on your strengths and accomplishments. Keep a journal of positive feedback and achievements to remind yourself of your capabilities. Look back at your journal regularly and you'll soon realize that you have so much more in your life than you first thought.

- **Take small risks:** Of course, that doesn't mean being reckless! Gradually step out of your comfort zone by taking small risks. Each successful experience will build your confidence and resilience, pushing you to take opportunities as they arise in the future. Besides, if it doesn't work out, simply learn from it, and go again.

Recognizing and overcoming self-doubt is essential for personal growth and well-being. However, remember that overcoming self-doubt is a journey, and the results won't happen overnight. You're going to need to be patient here; with every small win, celebrate, and move onto the next one. The effects are truly cumulative.

Building Self-Confidence & Self-Belief

Without self-confidence, you will never get anywhere in life. It's that simple. Self-confidence refers to having faith in your abilities, qualities, and judgment. It involves believing in yourself and feeling assured about your own worth and capabilities. Self-belief is closely related to self-confidence but specifically focuses on having a strong belief in your potential for success and achievement.

Both self-confidence and self-belief are essential for personal growth, happiness, and success. They enable you to overcome challenges, take risks, pursue their goals with determination, and handle setbacks or failures with resilience. Developing these qualities involves recognizing your strengths, setting realistic goals, embracing positive thinking patterns, practicing self-care and self-compassion, seeking support when needed, learning from experiences (both successes and failures), and continuously working on personal development.

It is important to note that building self-confidence and self-belief is a lifelong journey that requires effort and practice. Some situations in life will knock your confidence and you'll have to focus on building it up again. You're not born a confident person and you won't remain one throughout your whole life: it's about effort and self-reflection.

However, we do need to talk about the difference between self-confidence and arrogance. It's very easy to cross the line from being self-assured to being over-confident. This isn't an attractive trait, and it won't help you achieve your goals in life. It's important to know this so you don't go too far in your efforts.

Self-confidence and arrogance are two distinct traits, although they can sometimes be confused. So, let's outline the difference.

Self-confidence is a positive trait that stems from a belief in your abilities, skills, and worth. It involves having faith in yourself without feeling the need to belittle or dominate others. Self-confident people are secure in their own abilities but also respect and value the abilities of others.

On the other hand, arrogance is an excessive sense of self-importance or superiority over others. Arrogant people tend to believe they are better than everyone else and often display condescending behavior toward others. They may dismiss or devalue the opinions and achievements of those around them. As you can imagine, that doesn't lend itself to positive relationships in any sphere of life.

Your inner titan is confident and strong, but never arrogant.

Self-confidence is about having a healthy belief in yourself while still respecting others, whereas arrogance involves an inflated ego that disregards or diminishes the worth of others.

With that little word of warning out of the way, how can you build self-confidence and self-belief in today's fast-paced world?

- **Practice self-compassion**: Self-compassion involves treating yourself with kindness and understanding, especially in the face of setbacks or mistakes. Acknowledge that everyone is human and experiences imperfections. Instead of harsh self-criticism, offer yourself the same compassion and encouragement you would give to a friend in a similar situation. Embracing self-compassion helps build a positive and nurturing relationship with yourself, boosting self-confidence.
- **Set achievable goals**: Setting achievable and realistic goals is crucial for building self-confidence. Break down larger objectives into smaller, manageable tasks, and celebrate each milestone you accomplish. As you achieve these smaller goals, your confidence will grow, providing momentum to tackle more significant challenges.
- **Visualize success**: Visualization is a powerful technique to enhance self-belief. Take time to vividly imagine yourself succeeding in various situations. Whether it's acing a job interview or completing a challenging project, picturing yourself succeeding fosters a sense of self-assurance and prepares your mind for success.

- **Recognize and celebrate achievements**: Acknowledge your accomplishments and successes, no matter how small they may seem. Keep a journal of your achievements, and regularly review and celebrate them. This practice reinforces your self-belief and reminds you of your abilities during moments of doubt.

- **Face your fears and take risks**: Stepping outside your comfort zone is essential for building self-confidence. Identify your fears and take small, calculated risks to confront them. Each successful experience will bolster your belief in your capabilities and reduce the impact of self-doubt.

- **Develop competence**: Enhancing your skills and knowledge in areas of interest or professional development contributes significantly to self-confidence. Invest time in continuous learning, attend workshops, read books, or take courses that align with your goals. As you become more competent, your self-belief will naturally grow.

- **Surround yourself with supportive people**: Surround yourself with supportive and encouraging individuals who believe in your abilities. Positive influences can reinforce your self-confidence and offer valuable feedback and guidance when needed. Minimize interactions with people who undermine your self-belief or perpetuate self-doubt.

- **Learn from failure**: Failure is an inevitable part of life and viewing it as a learning opportunity rather than a reflection of your worth is crucial for building self-confidence. Analyze what went wrong, extract valuable lessons, and use them to improve and grow. Embracing failure as a stepping stone to success builds resilience and strengthens self-belief.

- **Practice positive self-talk**: Monitor your inner dialogue and replace self-doubting thoughts with positive affirmations. Remind yourself of your strengths, past accomplishments, and the progress you've made. Positive self-talk rewires your mindset and nurtures self-confidence.

- **Take care of yourself**: Physical and mental well-being play a significant role in building self-confidence. Prioritize self-care by getting enough sleep, engaging in regular exercise, and practicing relaxation techniques such as meditation or mindfulness. When you feel good physically and emotionally, your self-belief naturally improves.

Remember that self-confidence is not an innate trait but a skill that can be nurtured and developed over time, leading to a more fulfilling and empowered life.

Cultivating a Positive Self-Image & Embracing Personal Strengths

It should now come as no surprise that a positive self-image is a fundamental aspect of mental and emotional well-being. It involves having a healthy and confident perception of yourself, embracing individual strengths and qualities, and recognizing your inherent value.

Self-image refers to the mental and emotional picture you hold of yourself, including beliefs, attitudes, and perceptions about your identity, abilities, and worth. It is influenced by various factors, such as early experiences, social interactions, cultural background, and personal achievements. A positive self-image involves developing a constructive and compassionate view of who you are, where strengths and weaknesses are acknowledged without self-judgment.

Recognizing and embracing personal strengths is a crucial step in cultivating a positive self-image. Here are some effective techniques to start with:

- **Self-assessment:** Engage in self-assessment to identify your strengths, talents, and abilities. Reflect on activities and situations in which you have excelled or felt confident. Consider feedback from others that highlights your positive qualities.

- **Keep a strengths Journal:** Maintain a journal where you record instances when you demonstrated your strengths. Write about your achievements and positive traits, celebrating your successes regularly.

- **Seek feedback:** Seek feedback from friends, family, mentors, or colleagues. Their observations and insights can offer valuable perspectives on your strengths and potential areas for growth.

- **Accept imperfections:** We all have them! Understand that perfection is unattainable, and everyone has areas for improvement. Embrace your imperfections as part of being human and view them as opportunities for growth rather than inadequacies.

- **Celebrate achievements:** Celebrate your accomplishments, no matter how small they may seem. Recognize that every achievement, big or small, contributes to your personal growth and self-image.

Self-confidence that ebbs and flows throughout the course of life. It can be built up and knocked down in an instant, depending upon what comes your way. But just because you're going through a tough time or you're struggling to see the silver lining doesn't mean it's always going to be that way.

A huge part of the inner titan mindset is knowing that you're strong enough to overcome whatever life throws at you, because you believe in yourself.

Relying on others to believe in you doesn't work. You have to put in the work to believe in yourself in order to get anywhere. People will look at you and see a strong, confident person and want to be around them. That's much better than someone who struggles to see how great they are and always wants validation to be able to do anything.

You're not the latter, you're the former. And it's time you started believing it.

CHAPTER 10

Becoming a Leader For Yourself & Others

You might wonder why you need to become a leader if that doesn't describe your job. The thing is, leadership is about more than leading people in a particular role, it's about being a beaming light of guidance for those around you, while trusting yourself to do the right thing.

Leaders are strong people who others flock toward. They give you a sense of hope and confidence, while motivating you to move forward and better yourself. By developing your own leadership skills, you'll become that person.

Of course, self-discipline and effective leadership are intrinsically linked, as self-discipline forms the bedrock of a leader's ability to lead with purpose, focus, and integrity. Leadership requires guiding and motivating others toward shared goals, and this cannot be achieved without first mastering self-discipline.

In this chapter, let's explore the critical connection between self-discipline and effective leadership, and how the cultivation of self-discipline enhances leadership capabilities. All of this will help you to unleash your inner titan and become the kind of person that inspires others.

- **Leading by example**: Effective leaders lead by example, demonstrating the behaviors and qualities they expect from their team members or those around them. Self-discipline allows leaders to model consistency, commitment, and dedication, inspiring their team to follow suit. As a leader, if you demonstrate self-discipline in your actions, you create a culture of responsibility and accountability.
- **Resilience and decision-making**: Leaders face numerous challenges, and their ability to navigate through obstacles is directly linked to their self-discipline. Self-disciplined leaders remain composed and resilient under pressure, enabling them to make thoughtful and rational decisions even in high-stress situations. This capacity to stay focused and level-headed instills confidence in team members and encourages trust in their leader's judgment. It also gives you confidence when you see that your decision-making skills can be relied upon.
- **Time management and prioritization**: There are only so many hours in a day, and effective leadership involves juggling multiple responsibilities, tasks, and priorities. Self-disciplined leaders excel in time management, setting clear priorities, and staying focused on essential objectives. By efficiently allocating your time and attention, you optimize productivity and ensure that the team's efforts align with your goals.
- **Consistency in values and vision**: A self-disciplined leader operates with a clear sense of values and vision. They consistently act in alignment with these guiding principles, building trust and respect among team members. This steadfast commitment fosters a sense of purpose and direction, motivating people to work towards a shared vision.
- **Emotional intelligence and empathy**: Self-discipline plays a critical role in emotional intelligence, which is an essential aspect of effective leadership. Leaders with strong self-

discipline can manage their emotions and responses, making them more empathetic and approachable to their team. Within this, you have the ability to actively listen, understand different perspectives, and respond to team members' needs with composure and consideration.

- **Learning and adaptability**: Self-disciplined leaders embrace a growth mindset and are open to continuous learning and self-improvement. They are willing to adapt their strategies and approaches based on new information and changing circumstances. This adaptability allows you to lead effectively in dynamic environments and guide your team through challenges and transitions.
- **Accountability and ownership**: Effective leadership requires accountability and taking ownership of both successes and failures. Self-disciplined leaders are accountable for their actions and decisions, setting a precedent for responsible behavior within the organization. This means you acknowledge your mistakes, learn from them, and take proactive steps to rectify any issues that arise.
- **Building trust and followership**: The discipline demonstrated by a leader fosters trust and confidence among team members. When employees witness a leader's commitment to their own self-discipline, they are more likely to trust the leader's judgment and direction, leading to increased followership and loyalty.

Developing Leadership Qualities & Influencing Others

We've talked about leadership from a business point of view, but it's important to remember that leadership is not solely a position or title; it is a set of qualities and skills that inspire, guide, and influence others towards achieving common goals. Developing leadership qualities is a continuous process that requires self-awareness, adaptability, and a genuine desire to make a positive impact. That impact will reflect directly back on you.

Whether you're currently in a leadership position, you're aiming to be, or you simply want to learn how to develop leadership qualities, let's explore effective strategies for honing leadership qualities and mastering the art of influencing others:

- **Self-reflection and awareness:** Effective leadership begins with self-awareness. Take the time to reflect on your strengths, weaknesses, values, and leadership style. How do you communicate with people? What are your go-to habits? A journal may help you here. Understand your communication preferences, decision-making processes, and areas for improvement. By knowing yourself better, you can lead authentically and inspire trust in others.
- **Set clear goals and vision**: Developing leadership qualities involves having a clear sense of purpose and a compelling vision. Set ambitious yet achievable goals for yourself and your team. Communicate your vision in a way that ignites passion and commitment among your followers. A well-defined direction motivates others to rally behind your leadership.
- **Set a good example**: Leading by example is a powerful strategy for influencing others. Demonstrate the qualities and behaviors you expect from your team. Model integrity, accountability, and resilience. When your actions align with your words, you establish credibility and inspire others to emulate your behavior. After all, nobody will be inspired by a person who says one thing but does another. It doesn't show authenticity, so make sure you're always in alignment.
- **Communicate effectively**: Effective communication is at the core of influential leadership. Practice active listening, empathy, and clear expression of ideas. Tailor your

communication style to different individuals and situations, ensuring that your message resonates with your audience. It really comes down to taking the time to know the people around you and understanding how they react to different communication methods and strategies. This will help you get the best out of everyone.

- **Cultivate emotional intelligence**: Emotional intelligence (EI) is essential for understanding and connecting with others. Develop EI by recognizing and managing your own emotions and empathizing with the feelings of those around you. Emotionally intelligent leaders are better equipped to inspire and motivate their teams. EI also allows you to observe issues before jumping in and trying to solve them; it allows you to deal with situations much more calmly and effectively.
- **Encourage and empower others**: Great leaders empower their team members by recognizing their strengths and delegating tasks accordingly. Encourage open dialogue, value diverse perspectives, and provide opportunities for professional growth. A supportive and empowering environment fosters creativity and enhances team performance.
- **Build trust and rapport**: Trust is the foundation of any influential leadership. Be honest, reliable, and transparent in your interactions. Trust is earned through consistency, competence, and genuine concern for the well-being of your team members. This also links back to our earlier point of making sure that your words and actions align.
- **Develop decision-making skills**: Leadership requires making tough decisions. Sharpen your decision-making skills by gathering relevant information, considering the consequences, and seeking input from stakeholders when appropriate. Decisiveness inspires confidence in your leadership.

- **Be adaptable and resilient**: Leaders must navigate through challenges and uncertainties. Cultivate adaptability and resilience to handle unexpected situations with composure. Your ability to stay calm and composed in the face of adversity will inspire confidence and trust in your leadership. It will also inspire others to do the same.

Remember that leadership development is a lifelong journey. Stay committed to continuous learning and growth. Seek feedback, attend workshops, read books, and learn from other successful leaders. Embrace feedback as a tool for improvement and refinement of your leadership qualities. This isn't only for others either; it will enhance your life in ways you can't imagine.

Setting a Personal Example

Let's delve into this point a little more, since it's so important on many levels.

Leading by personal example is one of the most powerful ways to inspire and motivate others. When people see leaders living out their values, demonstrating resilience, and pursuing excellence, they are inspired to follow suit. So, how can you do that?

- **Authenticity and integrity**: Authenticity is key to inspiring others. When leaders live with integrity, staying true to their values and principles, they gain the trust and respect of their followers. Being genuine and transparent about both successes and challenges demonstrates authenticity and encourages others to do the same.

- **Setting high standards**: Leading by personal example involves setting high standards for yourself and others. When leaders continuously strive for excellence, they create a culture of achievement within the organization. Their commitment to quality work inspires their team to aim for greatness and achieve beyond expectations. However, that doesn't mean setting impossibly high standards; make sure you're not pushing yourself or others too far.

- **Demonstrating resilience**: Resilience in the face of adversity is a trait that inspires others to persevere. Leaders who handle setbacks and challenges with grace and determination set an example for their team. By showcasing resilience, you foster a positive and can-do attitude among your followers.
- **Embodying passion and enthusiasm**: Show your excitement! Passion and enthusiasm are infectious. Leaders who display genuine passion for their work and mission inspire others to share the same enthusiasm. Their excitement and energy can ignite a sense of purpose and dedication in their team members.
- **Celebrating successes and acknowledging efforts**: Sometimes a small "thank you" goes a long way. Recognizing and celebrating achievements, both big and small, is essential for motivating others. Leaders who acknowledge the efforts and successes of their team members create a positive and rewarding work environment. This positive reinforcement inspires individuals to continue striving for excellence.
- **Empowering and supporting others**: Inspiring leaders empower and support their team members. They believe in their employees' capabilities and provide them with the resources and autonomy to excel. By offering guidance and encouragement, you will foster a sense of ownership and self-belief in your team.
- **Practicing active listening and empathy**: Effective leaders listen actively and empathize with their team members' experiences and concerns. This empathetic approach creates a supportive and understanding work environment, making individuals feel valued and heard. Empathy builds trust and loyalty among team members, motivating them to contribute their best efforts.

- **Embracing lifelong learning**: Leaders who embrace a growth mindset and prioritize continuous learning inspire a culture of improvement and development. Your thirst for knowledge and curiosity encourages others to seek personal and professional growth, resulting in a more innovative and motivated team.
- **Demonstrating work-life balance**: A leader's ability to maintain a healthy work-life balance sets an important example for their team. Leaders who prioritize their well-being and demonstrate the importance of self-care inspire a healthier and more balanced approach to work and life among their followers.
- **Encouraging measured risk-taking and creativity**: Encouraging risk-taking and embracing creativity are crucial for inspiring innovation within the organization. Leaders who support experimentation and view failure as a learning opportunity foster a culture of innovation, inspiring their team to think outside the box and take calculated risks. However, that doesn't mean taking reckless risks; it means measured risks that have the potential for major gains.

Inspiring and motivating others through personal example is a transformative leadership approach that fosters a positive and high-achieving work environment. By following these tips as a leader, you can ignite a sense of purpose, dedication, and excellence within your team.

Remember that leading by personal example is not just about being a role model but also about positively influencing the lives of others, propelling them toward success, and nurturing a culture of continuous growth and achievement. All of this will benefit you and those around you, leading to stronger relationships and a more positive outlook.

The Things to Avoid as a Leader

Of course, within all of this, we should also talk about the things that a leader doesn't do, and the things you should avoid:

- **A leader doesn't shy away from taking responsibility:** They don't pass the blame onto others when things go wrong, but instead, they take ownership and work towards finding solutions.
- **A leader doesn't micromanage their team:** They trust their team members' abilities and delegate tasks accordingly, allowing them to take ownership of their work and showcase their skills.
- **A leader doesn't make decisions without considering the opinions and input of others:** They value collaboration and seek diverse perspectives to make well-informed choices that benefit the entire team or organization.
- **A leader doesn't ignore feedback or dismiss the ideas of others:** They actively listen to suggestions, concerns, and criticisms from their team members, recognizing that everyone's input is valuable for growth and improvement.
- **A leader doesn't prioritize personal gain over the success of the team or organization:** They understand that true leadership involves serving others, supporting their development, and fostering a positive working environment.
- **A leader doesn't avoid difficult conversations or conflicts within the team:** Instead, they address issues head-on with empathy and respect while seeking resolutions that benefit everyone involved.
- **A leader doesn't stop learning or growing professionally:** They continuously seek knowledge, stay updated on industry trends, and embrace new technologies or methodologies to adapt to changing circumstances effectively.

When learning how to lead others, it's very easy to go a little too far in the wrong direction and end up showing signs of poor leadership. Being aware of these issues means you can keep a check on your progress and avoid disaster.

CHAPTER 11

Embracing Adversity & Developing Grit

Life is strange. One minute everything is going wonderfully well, and then life throws you a curveball and everything is upside down. You're floundering, wondering which way to go, and not understanding where is up or down.

Yet, adversity, defined as challenges, difficulties, and hardships, is an inevitable part of life. While it may be uncomfortable and challenging to navigate, adversity plays a crucial role in personal growth and development. How you handle life's hurdles shapes who you are and what you do.

As much as you may not want to, it is through facing and overcoming adversities that you learn valuable life lessons, build resilience, and discover your true potential.

In this chapter, let's explore the significant role of adversity in personal growth and how it can shape you into a stronger, more capable individual. You just need to be brave and face it.

So, what are the plus points of facing adversity head on and literally saying, "Bring it on?"

- **Building resilience**: Adversity serves as a testing ground for resilience—the ability to bounce back from setbacks and difficulties. When you face adversity, you are forced to confront your fears, doubts, and limitations. By navigating through these challenges, you develop the strength and endurance to handle future difficulties with greater ease.

- **Promoting adaptability**: Adversity often requires you to adapt to new circumstances and find creative solutions to problems. Through adaptability, you learn to think critically, explore alternative approaches, and remain flexible in the face of change. This skill becomes invaluable in both personal and professional spheres.
- **Fostering problem-solving skills**: Adversity presents you with problems that demand innovative solutions. It encourages the development of problem-solving skills and encourages a growth mindset. Overcoming obstacles teaches you to be resourceful and approach challenges with a proactive attitude.
- **Cultivating empathy and compassion**: Experiencing adversity fosters empathy and compassion. Going through difficult times can help you understand the struggles others face and develop a deeper sense of empathy. This newfound compassion can lead to stronger connections with others and a desire to make a positive impact in the lives of those around you.
- **Enhancing self-awareness**: Adversity often forces you to look inward and examine your emotions, beliefs, and reactions to difficult situations. This process of self-reflection enhances self-awareness and promotes personal growth. Understanding your strengths and weaknesses enables you to make better-informed decisions and work toward self-improvement.
- **Encouraging personal transformation**: Adversity has the potential to be a catalyst for personal transformation. It can lead you to question your values, priorities, and life goals. During challenging times, it's normal to reevaluate your paths and make significant life changes to align with your true passions and aspirations.

- **Cultivating gratitude**: Adversity can provide a stark contrast that allows you to appreciate the positive aspects of your life. Going through tough times can foster gratitude for the things we often take for granted, such as good health, supportive relationships, and personal achievements.

- **Building confidence**: Overcoming adversity bolsters an individual's self-confidence. When individuals successfully navigate through difficult situations, they gain a sense of accomplishment and belief in their abilities. This confidence becomes a foundation for tackling future challenges with greater self-assurance.

- **Reinforcing determination**: Adversity tests an individual's determination and perseverance. Those who persist and stay committed to overcoming obstacles are better equipped to achieve their long-term goals. The experience of overcoming adversity reinforces the importance of persistence and staying focused on the journey ahead.

- **Inspiring others**: By facing adversity head-on and emerging stronger, individuals can inspire others to do the same. Sharing stories of resilience and personal growth can motivate and uplift those facing similar challenges, creating a ripple effect of empowerment within communities.

It's not easy to understand why we need to go through tough times in order to grow, but it's a reality. By understanding the role of adversity in personal growth, you can approach challenging times with a growth mindset and emerge from the experience stronger, wiser, and more resilient than before.

Techniques for Embracing Challenges & Developing Resilience

Even though challenges will always be difficult, resilience allows you to make it through to the other side much easier. Let's take a look at some strategies to help you develop this important life skill:

- **Reframe adversity as opportunities for growth**: Instead of viewing challenges as insurmountable obstacles, reframe them as opportunities for growth and learning. Embrace a growth mindset, recognizing that every difficulty provides a chance to develop new skills, gain wisdom, and become more resilient. Some of life's tougher challenges will obviously be more difficult, but once the ground has settled a little, look for the lesson in everything.

- **Develop a supportive network**: Build a network of supportive friends, family, mentors, or colleagues who can provide encouragement, understanding, and practical assistance during challenging times. Sharing your experiences and seeking support fosters a sense of connection and reduces feelings of isolation.

- **Practice positive self-talk**: Monitor your inner dialogue and replace negative self-talk with positive affirmations. Remind yourself of your strengths, past successes, and the resilience you have displayed in the past. Positive self-talk fosters a sense of self-belief and reinforces your ability to overcome challenges.

- **Cultivate emotional intelligence**: Emotional intelligence involves recognizing, understanding, and managing your own emotions and those of others. By developing emotional intelligence, you can navigate through challenging situations with greater composure and empathy, reducing stress and enhancing resilience. How do you do this? Through being positive, reframing negative events and thoughts, and seeing failures as learning opportunities.

- **Set realistic goals and celebrate progress**: Break down larger challenges into smaller, manageable goals. Celebrate each milestone you achieve, no matter how small, as it reinforces your progress and provides motivation to keep moving forward.

- **Cultivate Adaptability**: Life is unpredictable, and embracing change and uncertainty is a key aspect of resilience. Cultivate adaptability by staying open-minded, flexible, and willing to adjust your plans when necessary. Adaptability allows you to respond effectively to unexpected challenges and thrive in changing environments.

- **Practice Mindfulness and Self-Care:** Engage in mindfulness practices, such as meditation and deep breathing, to center yourself and manage stress. Prioritize self-care by getting enough rest, eating nourishing foods, and engaging in activities that bring joy and relaxation. A well-cared-for mind and body are better equipped to face challenges.

- **Learn from Past Experiences**: Reflect on past challenges you have overcome and the strategies you used to persevere. Draw upon these experiences as a source of inspiration and wisdom. Identifying what worked in the past can guide your approach to current challenges.

- **Develop Problem-Solving** Skills: Enhance your problem-solving skills by approaching challenges with a solution-oriented mindset. Break complex problems into smaller components, brainstorm potential solutions, and be willing to take calculated risks in pursuit of resolutions.

- **Practice Gratitude**: Cultivate gratitude by acknowledging and appreciating the positive aspects of your life. Focusing on what you are grateful for helps shift your perspective during challenging times, providing a source of strength and resilience.

Grit & Determination in the Face of Adversity

You don't only need resilience in life, you also need two other ingredients in the recipe: grit and determination.

Grit and determination are qualities that reflect a person's perseverance, resilience, and unwavering commitment towards achieving their goals.

Grit refers to the ability to maintain passion and sustained effort over a long period of time, even in the face of obstacles or setbacks. It involves having a strong sense of purpose and being willing to put in the necessary hard work and dedication to overcome challenges.

Determination, on the other hand, is the firmness of purpose or resolve to achieve something. It is about having a clear goal in mind and being willing to do whatever it takes to reach that goal. Determined people possess an unwavering belief in their abilities and are not easily discouraged by setbacks or failures.

Both grit and determination are essential qualities for success in any endeavor. They enable you to stay focused on your objectives, push through difficult times, learn from failures, adapt strategies when needed, and ultimately achieve your desired outcomes.

Developing both grit and determination can significantly impact your ability to overcome challenges, achieve success, and maintain a positive outlook during difficult times. So, let's look at how you can do exactly that:

- **Set clear and meaningful Goals**: Establishing clear, meaningful, and achievable goals provides a sense of direction and purpose. Identify what truly matters to you and set specific objectives that align with your values and aspirations. Meaningful goals act as powerful motivators, fueling your determination to face and overcome obstacles.

- **Develop a growth mindset**: Embrace a growth mindset, which is the belief that abilities and intelligence can be developed through effort and perseverance. Understand that setbacks and challenges are opportunities for learning and growth rather than indicators of failure. This mindset fosters resilience and encourages you to keep pushing forward despite setbacks.

- **Cultivate self-discipline**: Self-discipline is crucial for staying focused on your goals, even when faced with distractions or temptations to give up. Practice self-control in managing your time, energy, and resources. Create routines and stick to them, as consistency builds discipline and reinforces your determination to stay on track.

- **Embrace optimism**: Optimism does not mean denying the reality of adversity; rather, it involves maintaining a positive and hopeful outlook even in difficult circumstances. Focus on solutions rather than dwelling on problems. Cultivate optimism by reframing challenges as opportunities for growth and by visualizing successful outcomes.

- **Build a support system**: Surround yourself with a supportive network of friends, family, mentors, or colleagues. Seek advice, encouragement, and practical assistance when needed. Having a support system boosts your morale, reminds you that you are not alone in your journey, and strengthens your determination to persevere.

- **Learn from setbacks and failures**: View setbacks and failures as valuable learning experiences. Analyze what went wrong, identify areas for improvement, and apply the lessons learned to future endeavors. Embracing the growth that comes from failure fuels your determination to approach challenges with renewed insight and adaptability.

- **Practice resilience**: Develop resilience by acknowledging your emotions, seeking ways to cope effectively with stress, and focusing on solutions rather than dwelling on difficulties. Resilience helps you navigate through tough times with grace and determination.

- **Break challenges into smaller steps**: Large challenges can feel overwhelming, but breaking them down into smaller, manageable steps makes them more approachable. Tackling challenges incrementally allows you to build momentum and maintain a sense of progress, enhancing your determination to reach your ultimate goal.

- **Celebrate progress**: Acknowledge and celebrate your progress, no matter how small. Recognize the effort you put into overcoming challenges and use these achievements as fuel for your determination to keep pushing forward. Celebrating milestones fosters a sense of accomplishment and encourages you to continue persevering.

- **Find inspiration and role models**: Seek inspiration from individuals who have demonstrated grit and determination in their own lives. Learn from their stories, struggles, and successes. Having role models can motivate you to emulate their perseverance and determination in your own journey.

Cultivating grit and determination in the face of adversity is a transformative process that helps you to persevere, adapt, and thrive despite challenges. It will take time, but the journey is more than worth the end result.

How to Reframe Problems & Learn From Them

There are two ways to look at problems. You can allow them to drag you down and just give in, or you can tackle them head on regardless. No matter how bad the problem may seem, it will come to an end, and you can learn a lesson in the process. It might not seem that way while you're in the middle of it, but it's entirely possible to come out of that time with a renewed sense of positivity and hope.

Reframing problems in life and learning from them is a valuable skill that can help you grow and find solutions. Here are some steps to help you reframe problems and gain insights from them:

- **Shift your perspective:** Look at the problem from different angles or viewpoints. Try to see it as an opportunity for growth, learning, or a chance to develop new skills.
- **Identify the underlying emotions:** Understand how the problem makes you feel and acknowledge those emotions without judgment. This can help you gain clarity on what needs to be addressed.
- **Define the problem clearly:** Break down the problem into smaller components or specific aspects that need attention. This will make it easier to analyze and find potential solutions.
- **Seek alternative explanations:** Challenge your initial assumptions about the problem by exploring different explanations or interpretations of what might be happening. Consider other people's perspectives as well.
- **Brainstorm possible solutions:** Generate a list of potential solutions, no matter how unconventional they may seem at first glance. Encourage creativity and think outside the box.
- **Evaluate pros and cons:** Assess each solution's advantages, disadvantages, feasibility, and potential outcomes before making a decision on which one(s) to pursue further.
- **Take action:** Implement your chosen solution(s), while being open-minded about adjustments along the way if needed.

- **Reflect on lessons learned:** After addressing the problem, take time to reflect on what you have learned from this experience—both about yourself and how you approach challenges in general.
- **Seek support if needed:** Don't hesitate to reach out for guidance or support from friends, family members, mentors, or professionals who can provide fresh perspectives or advice when facing difficult problems.

Remember that reframing problems takes practice; it's not always easy but can lead to personal growth and resilience over time.

So, the next time that life throws you a curveball and it throws you right off course, employ what you've learned in this chapter, and you'll find that it doesn't push you too far away from where you need to be. Instead, you'll take a moment, regroup, and move forward with renewed determination and strength.

CHAPTER 12

Finding the Perfect Balance

Home and work-life balance refers to the equilibrium between your personal life and professional commitments. It is crucial because it allows you to maintain a healthy and fulfilling lifestyle while effectively managing your work responsibilities. Picture it as a set of scales perfectly balanced, without one side weighing down the other. That's what you need to aim for.

When you don't have this balance, another area of your life suffers. For instance, if you spend all your time at work, your personal life suffers, and you might have problems in your relationships. On the other hand, if you spend all your time at home, enjoying your personal life and not doing as much work as you should, your professional life will suffer, which can, in the worst cases, lead to loss of a job.

Here are a few reasons why home and work-life balance is important:

- **Mental well-being:** Balancing personal and professional life helps reduce stress, anxiety, burnout, and other mental health issues. It allows you to recharge, relax, and focus on your overall well-being.

- **Improved productivity:** When you have time for yourself outside of work, you are more energized, motivated, and focused during working hours. This leads to increased productivity as you can bring fresh perspectives and ideas to the table.
- **Stronger relationships:** Striking a balance between home life and work commitments enables you to spend quality time with family, friends, or engage in hobbies that nurture relationships outside of the workplace. This strengthens bonds with loved ones.
- **Enhanced physical health:** Maintaining a balanced lifestyle encourages regular exercise routines, healthy eating habits, sufficient sleep patterns—all of which contribute positively toward physical health.
- **Personal growth:** Having time for personal interests or pursuing hobbies outside of work fosters personal growth by allowing you to explore new skills or passions that may not be directly related to your career. You might even find that you discover a hobby that could take your career down a completely different path.
- **Increased job satisfaction:** Achieving a healthy balance between home life and work can lead to higher job satisfaction as it prevents feelings of being overwhelmed or constantly sacrificing personal needs for professional demands.

There is no set amount of time you should spend on each part of your life; everyone has a different idea of what balance means to them. What you should do is make sure that you're spending an equal amount on each part, and that nothing else is suffering as a result.

Achieving a Healthy Home & Work-Life Balance

It goes without saying that achieving a healthy balance can be difficult, so let's look at some ways you can make the process easier.

- **Set boundaries**: Establish clear boundaries between work and personal life. Define specific working hours and avoid bringing work-related tasks into your personal time. Similarly, set aside dedicated time for family, hobbies, and relaxation, and protect these periods from work-related interruptions.
- **Prioritize tasks and goals**: Identify your most important tasks and goals, both at work and in your personal life. Focus on completing high-priority tasks during designated work hours and avoid overcommitting to additional responsibilities that may encroach on personal time.
- **Learn to say no**: Be selective about taking on additional work or social commitments that can overwhelm your schedule. Learning to say no when necessary ensures you have enough time for yourself and your loved ones, promoting a healthier work-life balance.
- **Utilize time management techniques:** Implement time management techniques such as creating to-do lists, setting time limits for tasks, and using productivity tools. Effective time management can help you accomplish more in less time, freeing up space for personal activities.
- **Schedule regular breaks**: Incorporate regular breaks into your workday to rest and recharge. Short breaks throughout the day can enhance focus and productivity while reducing feelings of burnout. Use break times to engage in activities that promote relaxation, such as stretching or going for a short walk.
- **Separate your work space from your living space**: If possible, designate a specific area in your home for work-related

activities. Separating your work space from your living space helps create a mental boundary between work and personal life, allowing you to disconnect from work when you step away from your designated workspace.

- **Practice mindfulness and self-care**: Cultivate mindfulness practices such as meditation or deep breathing to manage stress and improve focus. Prioritize self-care activities that promote mental and physical well-being, such as exercise, hobbies, and spending quality time with loved ones.
- **Communicate with your employer**: Open communication with your employer about your work-life balance needs is crucial. Discuss flexible work options, remote work opportunities, or adjustments to your workload that can support a healthier balance between work and personal life.
- **Unplug from technology**: Set boundaries for technology use, especially during personal time. Avoid constantly checking work emails or messages outside of working hours. Unplugging from technology allows you to be present and engaged in your personal life without work-related distractions.
- **Plan and enjoy leisure time:** Schedule regular leisure time for activities you enjoy, whether it's spending time with family, pursuing hobbies, or engaging in recreational activities. Planning and dedicating time for leisure ensures you have moments of relaxation and joy to look forward to.

Nurturing Relationships While Staying Focused on Personal Goals

Balancing the pursuit of personal goals with nurturing meaningful relationships is a delicate and rewarding endeavor. Achieving success in both areas requires thoughtful planning, effective communication, and a commitment to maintaining a harmonious balance.

Let's take a look at some strategies to help you nurture your relationships while staying focused on your personal goals:

- **Define your personal goals**: Start by clearly defining your personal goals and priorities. Understand what you want to achieve and the timeline you have in mind. Having a clear vision of your objectives enables you to communicate your aspirations to your loved ones and align your efforts accordingly.
- **Communicate openly**: Open communication is key to nurturing relationships while pursuing personal goals. Discuss your ambitions and the effort required to achieve them with your partner, family members, and close friends. Be receptive to their feedback and concerns and encourage them to share their goals and aspirations as well.
- **Prioritize quality time**: Even when focused on personal goals, prioritize quality time with your loved ones. Set aside dedicated moments for family gatherings, date nights, or catching up with friends. Being present and engaged during these moments helps strengthen bonds and shows your commitment to nurturing your relationships.
- **Share your journey**: Share your journey toward personal goals with your loved ones. Update them on your progress, share your successes and challenges, and seek their encouragement and support. By involving them in your journey, you create a sense of togetherness and mutual understanding.
- **Be supportive of others**: Just as you seek support for your personal goals, be equally supportive of your loved ones in pursuing their aspirations. Show genuine interest in their endeavors, celebrate their achievements, and offer a helping hand when needed. Building a supportive environment strengthens your relationships and fosters reciprocity.

- **Set boundaries and manage time wisely**: Establish clear boundaries to strike a balance between personal time and time spent with loved ones. Effective time management is crucial in maintaining focus on your goals while still allocating sufficient time for your relationships. Prioritize tasks and limit distractions to optimize your time.
- **Cultivate empathy and understanding**: Cultivate empathy and understanding for your loved ones' needs and schedules. Recognize that they, too, may have personal goals and commitments. Being understanding of their own pursuits allows for a more harmonious coexistence of personal aspirations within relationships.
- **Celebrate milestones together**: When you achieve milestones in your personal goals, celebrate them with your loved ones. Recognizing and sharing your successes with those who care about you fosters a sense of unity and joy. Similarly, celebrate their accomplishments to strengthen your bond and demonstrate your support.
- **Practice active listening**: Engage in active listening during conversations with your loved ones. Show genuine interest in their thoughts and feelings and validate their experiences. Active listening creates stronger connections and promotes a deeper understanding of each other's perspectives.
- **Be flexible and adaptable**: Flexibility and adaptability are essential in balancing personal goals and nurturing relationships. Be willing to adjust your plans and schedules as necessary to accommodate the needs of your loved ones. Demonstrating flexibility shows your commitment to maintaining a harmonious relationship.

It's not really about having it all; it's about being able to do everything you want and setting boundaries to ensure that you don't go too far in one direction.

Successful navigation of this balance involves a continuous effort to prioritize both aspects of life and a willingness to adapt as circumstances evolve. If you can remain flexible, you'll notice that you maintain key relationships, develop new ones, and stay on track to achieve your goals in life.

Prioritizing Self-care & Maintaining Overall Well-being

Self-care is the intentional practice of taking care of your physical, emotional, and mental well-being and a vital aspect of leading a healthy and fulfilling life. Prioritizing self-care involves making time for activities and practices that promote overall well-being, reducing stress, and enhancing personal growth.

Of course, focusing on yourself when you've always been told to think of others can be difficult. With that in mind, let's explore the importance of self-care and provide effective strategies to maintain overall well-being.

Before we go on, let's look at why self-care is so important:

- **Physical health:** Self-care includes activities that support physical health, such as regular exercise, balanced nutrition, sufficient sleep, and medical check-ups. Prioritizing physical well-being enhances energy levels, strengthens the immune system, and reduces the risk of various health issues.
- **Emotional well-Being:** Self-care also encompasses emotional well-being. Engaging in activities that promote emotional health, like journaling, mindfulness, and seeking support from loved ones or professionals, can improve emotional resilience and coping skills.
- **Mental clarity:** Taking breaks, engaging in hobbies, and pursuing interests outside of work can improve mental clarity

and focus. Self-care activities help reduce mental fatigue and enhance creativity and problem-solving abilities.

- **Stress reduction:** Self-care serves as a powerful stress management tool. Activities like meditation, deep breathing exercises, and spending time in nature can reduce stress hormones, promote relaxation, and improve overall mood.
- **Personal growth:** Prioritizing self-care allows for self-reflection and personal growth. Engaging in activities that challenge and inspire us fosters a sense of accomplishment and boosts self-esteem.

Effective Strategies for Maintaining Overall Well-Being

If you're used to always focusing on work or other people, turning your attention to yourself might feel uncomfortable at first. After all, society tells us that we shouldn't be selfish and that we should always put others first. The problem is, when you do that, you're running yourself ragged and never stopping to fill up your energy reserves. How are you able to help others when you're not at your optimum level yourself?

Consider the airplane safety rule example: you're told to put your own life jacket on before helping others. Why? Because if you're about to drown or crash to the ground and die, you're not going to do very much for anyone else. But if you take the necessary steps to ensure your safety and well-being, you can turn your attention to helping others too.

The following strategies will help you focus on yourself without guilt:

- **Create a self-care routine**: Develop a self-care routine that includes activities for physical, emotional, and mental well-being. Allocate time for these practices regularly, making them a consistent part of your daily or weekly schedule.

- **Set boundaries**: Establish boundaries to protect your self-care time. Learn to say no to additional commitments when necessary and communicate your self-care needs to others.
- **Practice mindfulness**: Engage in mindfulness practices to stay present and focused. Mindfulness helps reduce anxiety and fosters a greater sense of contentment.
- **Engage in physical activities**: Incorporate regular physical activities that you enjoy, such as walking, yoga, dancing, or sports. Regular exercise not only improves physical health but also releases endorphins, enhancing mood.
- **Nurture social connections**: Make time for social interactions with friends, family, and loved ones. Strong social connections promote feelings of belonging and provide emotional support.
- **Get quality sleep**: Prioritize sufficient and restful sleep. Create a calming bedtime routine and aim for consistent sleep patterns to optimize physical and mental restoration.
- **Practice gratitude**: Cultivate a gratitude practice by expressing appreciation for the positive aspects of your life. Gratitude enhances overall well-being and cultivates a positive outlook.
- **Seek professional help when needed**: Don't hesitate to seek support from mental health professionals or counselors if you are experiencing emotional or psychological challenges.
- **Limit screen time**: Set limits on screen time, especially for activities that may contribute to stress or interfere with sleep, such as excessive social media or work-related tasks.

- **Be kind to yourself**: Practice self-compassion and avoid self-criticism. Treat yourself with the same kindness and understanding you would offer to a friend facing challenges.

Prioritizing self-care and maintaining overall well-being are essential for leading a healthy and fulfilling life. Remember that self-care is not a luxury but a necessary investment in your health and happiness, allowing you to show up fully for yourself and those around you.

CHAPTER 13

Embracing Discipline as a Lifestyle Choice

We've talked several times throughout this book about self-discipline and why embracing your inner titan cannot happen without it. Of course, self-discipline is the ability to control your impulses, actions, and emotions in pursuit of long-term goals and personal growth. It is a fundamental skill that allows you to overcome distractions, stay focused, and make consistent progress in various aspects of life.

However, sometimes self-discipline can be extremely difficult, but integrating it into everyday life is essential for achieving success, maintaining a balanced lifestyle, and fostering personal development.

Self-discipline is, in the end, a choice. You can choose to be disciplined and embrace it as a lifestyle, or you can just throw it out of the window and sit there lamenting the fact that things never seem to go your way. Of course, you're reading this book because your inner titan is begging to be released, so you're not going to go with the second option.

Here are a few pointers to help you embrace self-discipline as a long-term lifestyle choice:

- **Clarify your goals**: Start by identifying your short-term and long-term goals. Understanding what you want to achieve provides a sense of direction and purpose. Write down your goals and keep them visible to serve as a constant reminder of what you are working towards.
- **Develop daily routines**: Establish daily routines that align with your goals and priorities. Create a schedule that includes dedicated time for work, self-improvement, relaxation, and other essential activities. Following a routine helps minimize decision fatigue and promotes consistency in your actions.
- **Set specific, measurable, attainable, relevant, and time-bound (SMART) goals:** Transform your goals into SMART goals by making them Specific, Measurable, Attainable, Relevant, and Time-bound. This framework provides clarity and accountability, making it easier to stay disciplined in pursuing your objectives.
- **Practice time management**: Effective time management is crucial for self-discipline. Prioritize tasks based on their importance and deadlines. Use techniques such as the Pomodoro Technique (working in short, focused intervals) to enhance productivity and maintain focus.
- **Cultivate healthy habits**: Developing healthy habits strengthens self-discipline. Incorporate activities such as regular exercise, healthy eating, meditation, or journaling into your daily routine. Consistently practicing these habits builds self-control and resilience.
- **Limit distractions**: Identify and minimize distractions that can derail your focus. Create a conducive environment for work or study by reducing interruptions from social media, television, or unnecessary notifications.

- **Embrace delayed gratification**: Practice delayed gratification by resisting immediate rewards in favor of long-term benefits. Avoid impulsive decisions that may hinder your progress towards your goals. Cultivate patience and recognize that success often requires time and effort.

- **Take responsibility for your actions**: Accept responsibility for your choices and actions. Avoid making excuses or blaming external factors for setbacks. Acknowledging your role in the outcome empowers you to make better decisions and take corrective measures when necessary.

- **Visualize success**: Visualize yourself achieving your goals and living a disciplined, successful life. Positive visualization strengthens your determination and belief in your abilities, reinforcing your commitment to self-discipline.

- **Practice self-reflection**: Regularly reflect on your progress and assess whether you are staying true to your self-discipline efforts. Identify areas where you can improve and celebrate your achievements. Self-reflection helps you stay on track and maintain your commitment to personal growth.

- **Give yourself a break**: Remember that life is full of ups and downs and in the end, you're human. That means you're going to make mistakes and have days where you don't feel like pushing yourself as hard as you otherwise would. That's fine. Remember that self-care is just as important. The most important thing is that once you're recovered, you carry on in a disciplined way and don't allow pitfalls to push you off course for too long.

Integrating self-discipline into everyday life is a transformative process that requires dedication, consistency, and self-awareness. It won't always be easy, but the benefits are far-reaching. Also remember that self-discipline is a skill that can be developed and refined over time, and by incorporating these strategies into your daily life, you can unlock your full potential and lead a happier and healthier life.

Creating Daily Routines & Rituals to Support Discipline

Creating daily routines and rituals are useful methods to stay on track. These routines provide structure and consistency, helping you stay focused on your goals and aspirations. They serve as a guiding framework that empowers you to make intentional choices, cultivate positive habits, and build self-discipline over time.

Let's delve into the importance of daily routines and rituals and discover how they can contribute to a more disciplined and fulfilling life:

- **Find your rhythm**: Embrace your unique natural rhythm and identify the times of day when you feel most energized and focused. Tailor your daily routines to align with these periods. Whether you are a morning person or a night owl, structuring your day around your energy peaks enables you to make the most of your productive hours.

- **Start with small steps**: Begin by incorporating small, achievable routines into your day. Gradually build upon them as they become consistent habits. Starting with manageable tasks sets you up for success and prevents overwhelm, reinforcing your commitment to discipline.

- **Morning rituals for a purposeful start**: Establish a morning ritual that kick-starts your day with intention and positivity. Whether it's meditation, journaling, or exercise, engaging in activities that nourish your mind and body sets a positive tone for the rest of the day.

- **Set clear intentions**: Before starting your daily routines, set clear intentions for the day. Identify your top priorities and the tasks you need to accomplish. Having a sense of purpose provides direction and focus, keeping you on track to achieve your goals.

- **Include breaks and rest**: Incorporate breaks and moments of rest throughout your day to recharge and avoid burnout. Stepping away from work or responsibilities allows you to return with renewed energy and focus, contributing to a more sustainable and disciplined approach to your tasks.
- **Evening rituals for reflection**: Create evening rituals that foster self-reflection and gratitude. Review your accomplishments, acknowledge areas for improvement, and express gratitude for the positive aspects of your day. This reflection promotes self-awareness and encourages continuous growth.
- **Embrace flexibility**: While routines provide structure, it's essential to remain flexible. Life is unpredictable, and unexpected events may disrupt your plans. Embrace adaptability and respond to changes with a mindset of curiosity and resilience.
- **Accountability and support**: Share your daily routines and goals with a trusted friend, family member, or accountability partner. Having someone to support and encourage your efforts can keep you motivated and accountable to your commitment to discipline.
- **Celebrate your progress**: Celebrate your achievements, no matter how small. Acknowledge your efforts and the discipline it took to reach your milestones. Celebrating progress reinforces positive behavior and encourages you to continue on your disciplined path.
- **Remember self-compassion**: Be gentle with yourself when your routine doesn't go as planned. Life is filled with ups and downs, and it's normal to face challenges along the way.

Practice self-compassion and remember that discipline is a journey of growth and learning.

Your routines set the tone of your day and dictate your mindset to a large degree. By focusing on a positive set of routines, you're giving yourself a much better chance at a positive mindset. And when you're positive, the sky really is the limit.

Embracing Discipline as a Lifelong Journey of Growth & Self-Improvement

Discipline is not just a fleeting trait or a temporary practice; it is a profound and lifelong journey of growth and self-improvement. It encompasses the intentional cultivation of self-control, consistency, and determination to achieve personal goals and lead a purposeful life.

Understanding how discipline contributes to personal growth and self-improvement gives you a much better chance at moving forward in your life.

- **Understanding discipline as a mindset**: Embracing discipline starts with recognizing it as a mindset rather than a set of rigid rules. It involves adopting an attitude of commitment, resilience, and self-mastery. A disciplined mindset allows you to overcome challenges, resist temptations, and stay focused on your long-term aspirations.
- **Defining personal goals**: Discipline is deeply connected to having clear and meaningful goals. By defining personal goals and aspirations, you can align your actions and choices with your desired outcomes. These goals provide direction and purpose, acting as guiding beacons throughout the journey of discipline.
- **Cultivating consistent habits**: Discipline thrives in the cultivation of consistent habits. Engaging in positive

routines and rituals helps establish a strong foundation for self-discipline. By repeating beneficial behaviors regularly, individuals reinforce self-control and reinforce their commitment to personal growth.

- **Embracing self-awareness**: Self-awareness is a cornerstone of discipline. It involves recognizing personal strengths, weaknesses, and patterns of behavior. Embracing self-awareness enables you to identify areas for improvement and make intentional changes to achieve your goals.
- **Persevering through challenges**: Discipline empowers individuals to persevere through adversity and setbacks. When faced with obstacles, disciplined individuals do not give up easily. Instead, they view challenges as opportunities for learning and growth, enabling them to bounce back stronger.
- **Practicing continuous learning**: Discipline involves a commitment to continuous learning and improvement. Seeking knowledge, acquiring new skills, and remaining open to feedback contribute to personal development and the refinement of discipline.
- **Balancing self-Discipline with self-compassion**: While discipline is about self-control and determination, it is essential to balance it with self-compassion. Acknowledging that you are human and will make mistakes allows you to treat yourself with kindness and understanding. Self-compassion is not about excusing undisciplined behavior but about embracing your imperfections with grace and using them as opportunities for growth.
- **Celebrating progress and milestones:** Recognizing and celebrating the progress made along the journey of discipline is crucial. Small victories and milestones are important markers of personal growth. Celebrations reinforce positive behavior and motivate you to continue your disciplined efforts.

- **Adapting to change**: Discipline requires adaptability. Life is dynamic and constantly changing, and disciplined individuals must be willing to adjust their strategies and goals when necessary. Being adaptable ensures that discipline remains relevant and effective throughout life's different stages.
- **Viewing discipline as empowerment**: Ultimately, embracing discipline as a lifelong journey is an empowering endeavor. It allows you to take ownership of your life, steer your destiny, and actively shape your future. Discipline empowers you to lead a purposeful life and create positive impacts on yourself and those around you.

Being self-disciplined is a choice you have to make every day; it's a mindset, a commitment to personal goals, and the cultivation of consistent habits. Embracing discipline involves self-awareness, perseverance, continuous learning, and the practice of self-compassion.

Remember that discipline is a constant evolution, and every step taken toward self-improvement contributes to the broader picture of personal growth and fulfillment.

CHAPTER 14

It's Time to Unleash Your Inner Titan

We're now at the end of the book, how do you feel? Can you feel your inner titan pushing its way out of your mind? Can you feel yourself growing stronger with every second that passes?

The truth is that unleashing your inner titan isn't going to suddenly turn you into a force of nature. But what it will do is give you the strength and perseverance to overcome whatever life throws at you. It will allow you to believe in yourself and cultivate opportunities for progress. You'll have the confidence to take those opportunities and see where the road takes you.

It's an exciting time, for sure.

Remember that life is a journey filled with experiences, challenges, and opportunities for growth. Reflecting on your transformation and personal growth is a profound and enlightening practice that allows you to gain insight into your journey, acknowledge your progress, and appreciate the lessons you've learned along the way.

In this final chapter, let's delve into the significance of self-reflection, the power of personal growth, and the value of embracing change. Here are some tips and points to remember:

- **Embracing change as a constant**: Life is constantly evolving, and change is an inherent part of your existence. Reflecting on personal growth requires you to embrace change as a constant companion on your journey. By recognizing that growth often emerges from moments of change, you can welcome new opportunities and experiences with open arms.

- **Acknowledging milestones and achievements**: Self-reflection allows you to acknowledge and celebrate the milestones and achievements you've achieved during your transformation. Whether big or small, each success represents progress and deserves recognition. Celebrating these milestones reinforces your self-belief and motivates you to keep pushing forward.

- **Learning from challenges and setbacks**: Reflecting on personal growth involves embracing not only your successes but also your challenges and setbacks. It is through these difficult moments that you learn valuable lessons and build resilience. Understanding how you navigated through adversity enables you to approach future challenges with greater wisdom and strength.

- **Gaining self-awareness**: Self-reflection deepens your self-awareness, helping you understand your strengths, weaknesses, values, and motivations. This self-awareness enables you to make conscious choices aligned with your authentic self and empowers you to foster personal growth with intention.

- **Recognizing patterns of behavior**: By reflecting on your transformation, you can recognize patterns of behavior that may have hindered or propelled your growth. Identifying patterns allows you to break negative cycles and cultivate positive habits that support your personal development.

- **Appreciating growth as a process**: Personal growth is not a destination; it is an ongoing process. Reflecting on your journey reminds you that transformation is not an instant achievement but a gradual and continual evolution. Embracing this notion fosters patience and perseverance during moments of stagnation or slow progress.

- **Cultivating gratitude**: Reflecting on your personal growth evokes a sense of gratitude for the people, experiences, and opportunities that have influenced you positively. Gratitude nurtures humility and a deeper appreciation for the support and guidance you've received along the way.
- **Setting new goals**: Self-reflection inspires you to set new goals and aspirations based on your evolving understanding of yourself. It encourages you to dream bigger, reach further, and explore new possibilities for growth.
- **Sharing wisdom and inspiring others**: Reflecting on your transformation allows you to share your experiences and wisdom with others, inspiring and supporting them on their own personal growth journeys. By being open about your challenges and triumphs, you can create a ripple effect of empowerment and encouragement in your community.
- **Finding meaning and purpose**: Finally, self-reflection helps you find meaning and purpose in your experiences. Understanding how your journey has shaped you allows you to see the greater purpose behind your growth and inspires you to live a life that aligns with your values and passions.

Reflecting on transformation and personal growth is a powerful and enlightening practice. Through self-reflection, you deepen your understanding of yourself, celebrate your growth, and pave the way for continued personal development and fulfillment. Remember that transformation is a lifelong journey, and each moment of reflection contributes to the richness of your personal growth and the meaningfulness of your life.

Embracing Your Empowered Self & The Indomitable Spirit of Your Inner Titan

Within each of us lies a reservoir of untapped strength and potential, waiting to be harnessed and unleashed. This is the empowered self, a force of resilience, determination, and boundless courage that emerges when you embrace your true capabilities. Coupled with the indomitable spirit, this powerful combination becomes an unstoppable force that propels you through life's challenges and toward your dreams.

You might not recognize this part of you right now, but you're already on the right track. The empowered self is born when you shed the limitations you place upon yourself and liberate your mind from self-doubt and fear. It is a realization that you have the power to shape your destiny and create the life you envision. The moment you embrace this empowered self, you break free from the chains that have held you back and begin to soar to new heights.

Embracing the empowered self is not about being fearless; it is about acknowledging your fears and pushing forward despite them. It is about taking risks and stepping outside your comfort zone to embrace growth and change. It is about recognizing that failure is not an end but a step toward success. With each stumble, you learn, grow, and become even more powerful than before.

But the empowered self cannot thrive without the indomitable spirit. The indomitable spirit is the unyielding force that drives you forward, even in the face of adversity. It is the fiery passion that ignites your soul and fuels your determination. It is the unwavering belief that you can overcome any obstacle that stands in your way.

The indomitable spirit does not waver in the face of setbacks or challenges. It does not succumb to doubt or despair. Instead, it rises from the ashes of defeat and emerges stronger and more resilient than ever before. It draws its strength from a deep well of inner courage and an unshakable belief in your abilities.

Together, the empowered self and the indomitable spirit create a formidable alliance. They become the driving force behind your dreams, pushing you to strive for greatness and persevere through the darkest of times. They allow you to embrace your authenticity and boldly chase after what sets your heart on fire.

In times of doubt or uncertainty, remember the power that resides within you—the strength to overcome, the courage to face your fears, and the determination to triumph over any obstacle. Embrace the empowered self and awaken the indomitable spirit that dwells within.

Of course, this is not a one-time event but a continuous journey. It requires a commitment to self-discovery, growth, and embracing challenges with an unwavering belief in yourself. As you walk this path, inspire others to do the same, lighting a beacon of hope for all who may feel lost or discouraged.

So, now you have all the information you need to stand tall, confident in your abilities, and unyielding in the pursuit of your dreams. Embrace the empowered self and the indomitable spirit; they are the keys to unlocking your fullest potential and living a life of purpose and passion.

You can rise above any obstacle, conquer any fear, and make your mark on the world. You just need to believe in your own abilities. Embrace the empowered self and ignite the indomitable spirit within you. Trust me, the possibilities that await are limitless.

Final Thoughts & Encouragement For Unleashing Your Inner Titan

The journey to unleash your inner titan may not always be easy. You will face challenges, doubts, and moments of uncertainty. But remember, every great titan faced obstacles on their path to glory.

Embrace each challenge as an opportunity to grow stronger and wiser.

Believe in yourself with unwavering faith. Doubt has no place in the heart of a titan. When you believe in your abilities and trust in your vision, the universe conspires to make your dreams a reality.

- **Do not let the opinions of others deter you:** Titans are not swayed by the judgments of the crowd. Stay true to your purpose and walk your own path with confidence and conviction.
- **Harness your passions and channel them into relentless determination:** Let your dreams fuel the fire within, igniting an unquenchable thirst for success. You are the master of your destiny, and with each step, you are shaping a future of triumph and achievement.
- **Embrace failure as a stepping stone toward greatness:** Titans do not fear stumbling; they rise stronger with each fall. Learn from your mistakes, for they are the building blocks of wisdom and resilience.
- **Surround yourself with those who lift you higher:** As well as those who believe in your vision, and who inspire you to be your best self. In the company of like-minded individuals, you will find the support and encouragement to conquer any challenge.
- **Be relentless in the pursuit of growth and self-improvement:** Titans are never stagnant; they are always evolving and expanding their horizons. Continuous learning and self-discovery will propel you to new heights of greatness.
- **Above all, remember that unleashing your inner titan is not a destination but an ongoing journey:** Embrace the process, savor the victories, and learn from every experience. Each day is an opportunity to become a better version of yourself, a more powerful and empowered titan.

As you unleash your inner titan, you will inspire others to do the same. Your courage, determination, and indomitable spirit will ignite a spark in the hearts of those around you.

Now, the time has come to unleash your full potential and conquer the world. Embrace the power within you and always remember that you are destined for greatness. Let your light shine brightly and inspire others to do the same.

Go forth with courage, passion, and unwavering belief in your abilities. Unleash your inner titan and let your indomitable spirit soar!

REFERENCES

8 Amazing benefits of Meditation. (n.d.). Wildwood Ridge Apartments. https://www.wildwoodridgeapartments.com/Portal/Home/BlogPost/9bb8daed-1949-47cc-8389-adb8688bb364

Amar, S. (2016, November 18). *Swati amar.* https://blog.ijugaad.com/stay-positive-stay-happy/

Ambaya Gold Health Products. (n.d.). *Easy New Year's resolutions for health.* https://ambayagold.com/blogs/news/top-new-years-resolutions-for-health

Annabel. (2021, July 8). *journal prompts.* Inspiring Tips. https://inspiringtips.com/asia/tag/journal-prompts/

Appliedalliance. (2018, January 24). *With courage.* Appliedalliance. https://appliedalliance.wordpress.com/2016/07/31/expanding-your-horizons/

Blog. (2017, December 29). Tarla Makaeff. https://tarlamakaeff.com/blogs/online-marketing/tagged/fear-of-failure

Blouin, J. (2023). The Power of Discipline: How it Can Help You Achieve Your Goals and Live Your Best Life. *Julie Blouin.* https://julieblouin.com/the-power-of-discipline-how-it-can-help-you-achieve-your-goals-and-live-your-best-life/

Burns, S. (2022, December 31). Neuroscientists Explain How to Have An Edge Over Others (Scientific Trick) - New Trader U. *New Trader U.* https://www.newtraderu.com/2022/12/31/neuroscientists-explain-how-to-have-an-edge-over-others-scientific-trick/

Chakraborty, S. (2023). How to overcome tiredness and boost energy levels? *Roseatehouselondon*. https://roseatehouselondon.com/how-to-overcome-tiredness-and-boost-energy-levels/

Coronary heart disease - Public health portal - Bracknell Forest Council |. (2018, April 16). Public Health Portal - Bracknell Forest Council |. https://health.bracknell-forest.gov.uk/self-care-guide/coronary-heart-disease/

Delrecruiters. (2023, May 9). *Secrets to keeping employees happy without a raise - Delrecruiters*. Delrecruiters. https://www.delrecruiters.com/secrets-to-keeping-employees-happy-without-a-raise/

Faith, family, fitness. (n.d.). https://www.cynthiawenz.com/the-cynopsis/faith-family-fitness

Getting Through Tough Times with Resilience. (n.d.). https://lifeism.co/getting-through-tough-times-with-resilience

Goal Setting and WHY it is so Important. (n.d.). https://www.homepreneursclub.com/blog/goalsetting

HBB Trends. (n.d.). *Healthy living*. https://hbbtrends.com/products/healthy-living

How to build an action plan to reach your goals | Gloveworx. (n.d.). Gloveworx. https://www.gloveworx.com/blog/how-build-action-plan-reach-your-goals/

How to manage stress? (2021, October 29). CMR. https://en.centrodemedicinaregenerativa.com/post/how-to-manage-stress

Hutchinson, D. (2022, December 15). *Why Is It Important To Set Health Related Goals - Health and Fitness Tips*. Health and Fitness Tips. https://healthandfitnesstips.us/why-is-it-important-to-set-health-related-goals/

I need help developing healthier habits for managing stress. (n.d.). https://www.emergentmind.com/posts/i-need-help-developing-healthier-habits-for-managing

Inal, Y., & Inal, Y. (2022, October 5). How to be productive Without getting stressed out - ProductiveMuslim.com. *ProductiveMuslim.com - Meaningful Productivity That Connects This Life With The Hereafter.* https://productivemuslim.com/getting-stressed-out/

Increasing Happiness–Scientifically. (2020, January 2). Surviving Mexico. https://survivingmexico.com/2017/11/27/increasing-happiness-scientifically/

January 2015 - The Mediation Center. (2015, January 22). The Mediation Center. https://mediationctr.com/2015/01/

Jesse. (2023, January 24). *The Science Behind Gamified Assessments – janiorestaurant.* https://janiorestaurant.com/general/the-science-behind-gamified-assessments/

KaziHealth lifestyle interventions | KaziBantu. (n.d.). https://www.kazibantu.org/news/lifestyle-interventions/

Kitari, A. (2022). What exactly are triggers anyway? *Empowered With Alana.* https://empoweredwithalana.com/shadow-working/what-exactly-are-triggers-anyway/

Lam, C. (2022, November 28). *Two Techniques For Building Resilience During Divorce - Divorce Lawyer - Toronto Family Lawyer.* Divorce Lawyer - Toronto Family Lawyer. https://benmor.com/build-resilience-during-divorce/

Lee, D. H., Reasoner, K., & Lee, D. (2021). Grit: what is it and why does it matter in medicine? *Postgraduate Medical Journal, 99*(1172), 535–541. https://doi.org/10.1136/postgradmedj-2021-140806

LifePoint. (2021). The Truth about Self-Care. *LifePoint Church.* https://resources.lifepointchurch.us/the-truth-about-self-care/

Lifting Your Mood Through Activity | The British CBT & Counselling Service. (n.d.). The British CBT Counseling Service. https://www.thebritishcbtcounsellingservice.com/lifting-your-mood-through-activity-part-1/

Lingo, T. (2023). Using past failures as learning toward future success. *TeacherLingo.com*. https://teacherlingo.com/using-past-failures-as-learning-toward-future-success/

Lisa, A. (2023, January 3). *Selecting The Right Healthy Meal Delivery Service – autonewshr*. https://www.autonewshr.com/general/selecting-the-right-healthy-meal-delivery-service/

Macias, C. (2023, April 4). The importance of Self-Care and Self-Compassion for breathwork instructors. *Soup.io*. https://www.soup.io/the-importance-of-self-care-and-self-compassion-for-breathwork-instructors

McKenna, H. (2023, April 2). The Importance of Interpersonal Skills in Leadership | Sounding Board Inc. *Sounding Board Inc*. https://www.soundingboardinc.com/blog/leadership-capability-interpersonal-skills/

Negi, C. (2023). 10 best tips on how to overcome adversity. *TheStartupBusinessGuide*. https://thestartupbusinessguide.com/how-to-overcome-adversity/

Pradeepa, S. (2023). 8 Types of Self-Confidence: 7 Easy Ways to Build it. *Believe in Mind*. https://www.believeinmind.com/self-growth/types-of-self-confidence/

Ray, A., & Ray, A. (2023). The power of Motivational Speakers for mompreneurs. *Bugs Moran*. https://www.bugsmoran.net/the-power-of-motivational-speakers-for-mompreneurs/

Sabith, Sabith, & Sabith. (2023). Maximizing Productivity in HR: Strategies for running an Efficient department. *Famavip.com -*. https://famavip.com/maximizing-productivity-in-hr-strategies-for-running-an-efficient-department/

SHEROES - The Women-Only Social Network. (n.d.). https://sheroes.com/articles/10-creative-ways-to-overcome-stress-at-workplace/MTY4NDM

Snyder, L. (2023). Unlocking Your Potential. How To Overcome 3 Key Barriers to Achieve Your Goals. *Lori K. Snyder.* https://loriksnyder.com/unlocking-your-potential-how-to-overcome-3-key-barriers-to-achieve-your-goals/

Soulwarrior. (2023). How to become fearless. *Soul Warrior Wealth & Tarot.* https://soulwarriortarot.com/how-to-become-fearless/

Team, A. (2023). How to accomplish your goals in 2023. *VADE Nutrition.* https://vade-nutrition.com/blogs/news/goals-how-to-set-measure-and-accomplish-goals-in-2023

Team, O. (2022, January 14). *Making Blue Monday Brighter – OptiMe.* https://optimewellbeing.com/2022/01/14/blue-monday-2/

The link between exercise and diabetes management. (n.d.). https://www.mykindaplace.com/the-link-between-exercise-and-diabetes-management/

Thebels. (2022, December 29). Survival mode: When you were raised in survival mode, you see the world differently. *All about health, psychology and beauty.* https://www.netaveiro.com/2022/12/survival-mode.html

Thomas, V. a. P. B. C. (2022, October 21). *Behaviour change: if it's so 'easy', why do so many studies show it won't last?* Heart Sisters. https://myheartsisters.org/2021/10/10/behaviour-changes-dont-last/

Virily, A. (2022). 5 ways to reduce stress for a healthier life. *ELMENS.* https://www.elmens.com/lifestyle/5-ways-to-reduce-stress-for-a-healthier-life/

what brain fog feels like? (2022, March 18). LabElymental. https://www.themilkcleanse.com/blogs/reference-guide/what-brain-fog-feels-like

Winbolt, B. (2023). “How can I be calmer in any situation?” *Barry Winbolt.* https://www.barrywinbolt.com/how-to-be-calmer/

Made in United States
Cleveland, OH
02 January 2025